# FIRST OF THE MANY

*By the same author*

BLOODY APRIL

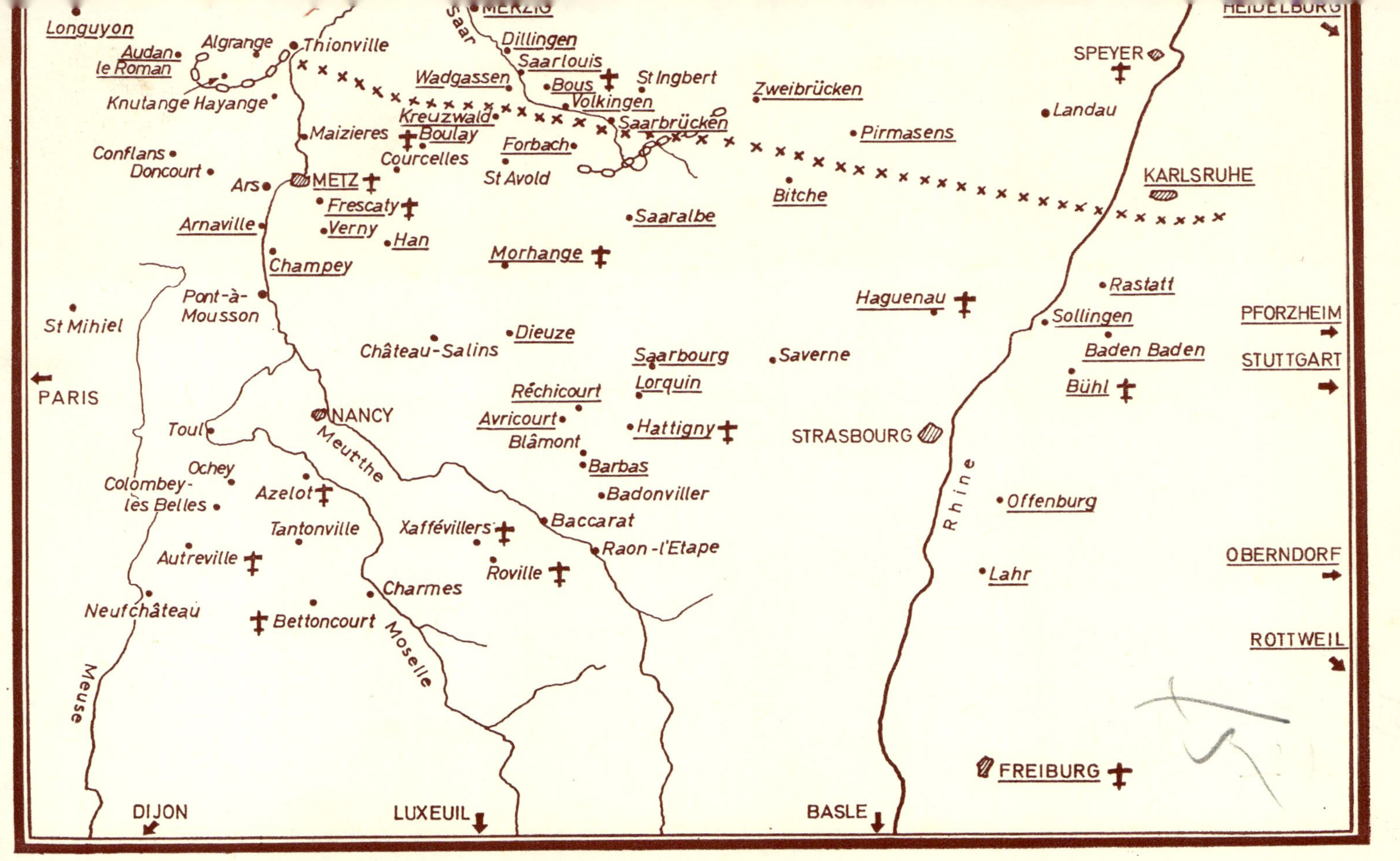

Longuyon
Audan
le Roman
Algrange
Thionville
Knutange Hayange
Saar
Dillingen
Saarlouis
Wadgassen
Bous
Volkingen
St Ingbert
Zweibrücken
SPEYER
Landau
Kreuzwald
Boulay
Maizieres
Saarbrücken
Pirmasens
Conflans
Doncourt
Courcelles
Forbach
St Avold
Ars
METZ
Bitche
KARLSRUHE
Frescaty
Verny
Han
Arnaville
Saaralbe
Morhange
Champey
Rastatt
Haguenau
Sollingen
Baden Baden
PFORZHEIM
STUTTGART
St Mihiel
Pont-à-Mousson
Dieuze
Château-Salins
Saarbourg
Saverne
Lorquin
Bühl
PARIS
Réchicourt
Avricourt
Blâmont
NANCY
Toul
Hattigny
STRASBOURG
Meutthe
Barbas
Badonviller
Ochey
Colombey-lès Belles
Azelot
Rhine
Offenburg
Baccarat
Tantonville
Xafffévillers
Raon-l'Etape
Autreville
Roville
OBERNDORF
Lahr
Charmes
Neufchâteau
Bettoncourt
Moselle
ROTTWEIL
Meuse
FREIBURG
DIJON
LUXEUIL
BASLE

Alan Morris

# FIRST OF THE MANY

*The story of Independent Force, RAF*

JARROLDS

JARROLDS PUBLISHERS (LONDON) LTD
*178–202 Great Portland Street, London W1*

London Melbourne Sydney
Auckland Bombay Toronto
Johannesburg New York

*First published 1968*



*This book has been set in Plantin, printed in Great Britain on Antique Wove paper by Anchor Press, and bound by Wm. Brendon, both of Tiptree, Essex*

09 087360 2

*To Dorothy*

## *Squadron Song*

I want to go to Essen
To drop my little egg.
The Kaiser, he thinks it
Out of my reach;
Somebody's pulling his leg.
I want to go to Essen
To call on Fräulein Krupp.
My DH9A will come back
All the way;
And the Kaiser will have
The wind up!

(*written by Major H. R. Nicholl,* CO, *110 Sqn.*)

# Contents

# Illustrations

*Between pages 84 and 85*

# Foreword

by

AIR MARSHAL SIR ROBERT SAUNDBY

KCB, KBE, MC, DFC, AFC, DL

*Deputy Commander-in-Chief, Bomber Command 1943–5*

The first of the many were those very gallant pilots, observers and air gunners of the Independent Force, supported by their hard-working and long-suffering air mechanics, who during the last year of the First World War flew on strategic missions over Germany. With imperfect aircraft, unreliable engines, and primitive flying instruments, they flew by day and by night, often at considerable heights and in appalling weather. They had no closed cockpits, no effective heating, no self-sealing tanks, and no parachutes. Because they knew little or nothing of these things, they cheerfully carried on without them. Though their casualty rate was high, their worst trials were not the running fights against the enemy's air defences, but failing engines and cruel weather.

In the vivid and stimulating pages of this book can be seen all the problems, in embryo, which Bomber Command had to solve. Allowing for the difference in scale and technical development, there are many striking similarities between the story of the Independent Force and the story of Bomber Command.

Through a long year of frustration and high endeavour this small company of pioneers not only made history, but laid the foundations on which was built the great strategic bombing campaign of the Second World War. It is fitting that the saga of their deeds and sacrifices should be made known as widely as possible.

Above all, we can look back on the first of the many with admiration and pride for their valour and determination. Just as our fighter pilots in the Battle of Britain were inspired by the exemplary courage and daring of the 'scout' pilots of the RFC, so our overstrained bomber crews in the Second World War were heartened and sustained by the splendid traditions of the Independent Force.

R. Saundby

# Take-off

As he stooped The Stranger felt the heat climbing to him from the summer-baked soil of the aerodrome. With it was wafted the sickliness of old oil, still matting the flattened brown grass and making a mould of tyre ruts imprinted by machines of three Royal Air Force squadrons.

For this was Azelot, just too far from the Vosges hills to benefit from their shadow. Here, six months before, the biplane bombers with flapping fabric and sighing wires had fluttered to rest like moths weary from their tussle with the winds and the winged predators.

Here an American subaltern named Philip Dietz had swung a de Havilland 9 on take-off and demolished a hangar; here Sgt Pilot Wilson had stalled, killing himself and 2nd Lieut H. E. Alsford; here the bleeding Hunters and Swanns had been hauled from their cockpits slashed by anti-aircraft shell and Maxim bullet; here groundlings such as Cpl Wymark had crumpled under steel rained by retaliatory German raiders.

Here their friends had slept fitfully. Just beyond the perimeter in the Croix Rouge rest room run by Mrs Huntington and Miss Studholme they had borrowed books recalling the recent past of their boyhood. In the adjoining odorous French village they had drunk wine to forget the present. Their future they left in hands marking maps several kilometres away.

So in 1918 it was at half a dozen British aerodromes semicircling Nancy, capital of the Departement de Meurthe-et-Moselle, 220 miles east of Paris, a dozen from No-Man's-Land.

The Stranger pocketed the dirt-caked Walker looseleaf diary he had picked up and left the arena to the ploughs of peasants stolidly reclaiming their land along the boundary.

On June 9, 1919, a British aero publication ran a personal item . . .

A reader wished to return the book to its owner, whose signature had been deciphered as 'G. Little'. The journal believed an officer of that name—actually 2nd Lieut J. E. Little of 55 Sqn—had served at Azelot. Then, venturing a further clue, it observed that the diary had been recovered from a camp abandoned by the IAF (*Indian* Air Force).

That translation was not even half right. 'Indian' should have been Independent; and, despite the colloquial style used by its personnel, the 'Independent Air Force' was not an air service. Indeed it was merely a part of the new and controversial RAF, and so little publicised that a year after its creation its true title could be confused by aviation experts.

As the Independent Force, RAF, however, from July to early November in 1918 it had dropped bombs weighing a total of 558 tons in numerous raids on German territory, more than a third of which were flown during daylight against overwhelming odds and over distances then unequalled by aeroplanes.

Many of its missions were undertaken by freezing crews sick with influenza, oxygen lack, and poisonous fumes, in faulty machines, and through acres of wet cloud.

Never more than nine operational squadrons strong, physically the Force was enfeebled by casualties mounting in battle alone to a peak of 75 per cent. Yet their Commander's deadliest foes were in the rear:

Politicians lusting after 'eye-for-an-eye' tactics, militarily inept but immediately satisfying to voters; supply departments providing dangerous equipment, and even that tardily; Allied Army chiefs hating the autonomy, at least nominal, of the unique Cinderella.

While thus engaged front and rear the Independent Force became the Royal Air Force-in-embryo, the world's first air weapon divorced from Army or Navy; the first organisation to undertake regular and systematic strategic bombing; and the forerunner of the British Bomber Command and of the US Strategic Air Force.

Its potential was enormous. Had World War I lasted a few hours more the Force would have bombed Berlin from Britain and might—who can be definite?—have diverted Germany from the collision course she set ten years later. Certainly it was only weeks away from becoming the nucleus of the first international air arm, which would have brought the horrors of day-long bombardment home to every important town in the Fatherland.

When a French general questioned the Force's title—'Independent of whom? Of God?'—he intended an insult. Six months passed before the words sounded like homage.

* * *

Neither squadron records nor log-books, scrawled by tired men heedless of history because they were too busy making it, can tell the whole story. My first duty, therefore, is to those of that notable band of brothers who, with youthful enthusiasms unimpaired, have recalled for me the sights and sounds and smells associated with working a stick-and-wire bomber deep inside enemy territory.

In this respect I wish particularly to thank Mr William W. Tanney (55 Sqn) of Detroit, Michigan, for his reminiscences and valuable suggestions about sources in the United States; Mr Leslie R. Blacking, for unstinted help and background on Handley Page characteristics; Mr A. J. Linnell, brother of Mr Geoffrey Linnell (216 Sqn); Mr Cyril Box (115 Sqn), whose immaculate training notes remain a fine example for any cadet; and Group Captain Robert Halley, DFC, AFC (216 Sqn), the only pilot to bomb from a Handley Page V/500—at Kabul on May 24, 1919, during the Third Afghan War.

I am also indebted to Captain William Armstrong, AFC (110 Sqn) for the photograph of his aircraft, the jingles of Waterous and Nicholl, and permission to quote from his fascinating *Pioneer Pilot* (Blandford Press); to Andrew Boyle, for quotations from his biography, *Trenchard, Man of Vision* (Collins); and to William Heinemann Ltd for similar courtesies in connection with Maurice Baring's *Flying Corps Headquarters 1914–18*.

Major W. F. J. Harvey, MC, DFC, TD, has been a constant and zealous guide to 1918 flying practice; and the late Air Vice-Marshal Sir Raymund Hart delved into his unrivalled knowledge of technical aspects.

Any thanks to Captain W. E. Johns (55 Sqn) must be inadequate. On the personal plane he accepted my first writings for his *Popular Flying* and *Flying* magazines which, sadly, have no modern counterparts. But I cannot express the Nation's debt to his 'Biggles' books, which encouraged thousands to join the Auxiliary Air Force and RAF Volunteer Reserve or to acquire an A

Licence in time for September 1939. These, together with his mid-thirties advocacy—often impish but always unmistakable—of an appropriate strategic bomber force can never be properly rewarded.

Through these men and their works I acquired deep respect for the gay gallantry of the IF, which they persist in calling 'Independent Air Force' and which, in the light of the influence it exerted on strategists' thought if not action, seems not too grand a title.

Their co-operation has been reinforced by the unfailing diligence of Mr. Vernon Rigby and Mr E. C. H. Hine of the Imperial War Museum (whose files provided all but one of the photographs), and by the lively interest of Sqn Ldr Humphrey Wynn of *Flight International*.

The interpretation of events is my own and if somewhere the innumerable flying wires have become entangled that fault is mine also.

AM

# PHASE I

## *'Eye for an eye . . .'*

# I

*'... He will not be slack to him that hateth him, he will repay him to his face.' (Deut 7:10)*

There were 20 of them, facets of a diamond whose full lustre was subdued against the mottled grey sky at 10,000 feet. They followed the River Crouch, skirted Rochford, and at Tottenham veered to pass across London from the north-west. Saturday-morning shoppers remarked their neat formation and felt a warm pride in the skill of British fliers. Some were waving when the first bombs swished down...

One missile struck the Central Telegraph Office, another the quadrangle of Ironmongers' Hall. Others hit warehouses, churches, and houses; but acres of shattered slates and windows were partly the consequence of 70 anti-aircraft guns firing 3233 ineffective shells. Fifty-seven people were killed, 193 wounded. Despite being sought, and rarely assailed, by 95 pilots—James McCudden, the Empire's top-ranking ace, among them—only one of the German intruders, a Gotha G IV, fell to Royal Flying Corps and Royal Naval Air Service interceptors.

Nevertheless, this engagement on July 7, 1917, was to prove incalculably costly to the German nation. From that date there was no doubt that the Fatherland, so far merely pin-pricked, would experience total war.

A signal recommending reprisal bombing reached the one man who might help: a stormy, stubborn, Anglo-Scot named Hugh Trenchard, then a Major-General and the RFC's chief with the British Expeditionary Force in France and Belgium. A paradox, at once an inarticulate 'regimental' figure and a vigorously practical visionary, Trenchard had outfought the Imperial German Air Force during the Somme and Arras battles.

He now replied that the bombing of London could only be

stopped by knocking out the German aviation where it lived, in the Occupied zones. However, when a squadron with reliable engines was made available he would 'strongly recommend'—Field Marshal Sir Douglas Haig, the BEF commander, being literally a stumbling block—the bombing of factories at Mannheim.

From this cautious opinion Trenchard, embittered by three years of doing without, making do, improvising, and generally suffering the false optimism of Government supply departments, would not budge.

When necessary he did not spare his young men but he would not sacrifice them to solve a political problem. He had always wanted to hammer the enemy's industrial might but only when results could outweigh the costs; a philosophy which precluded any diminution of the Army's strength in the field.

Strategic bombing was not a new notion. It had been practised intermittently by both sides since 1914 and the lessons were plain to Trenchard.

The effects in no way promised an important, let alone a decisive, outcome. Neither Rumpler Taube monoplanes over Paris nor Zeppelins over the length of eastern Britain had done more than create momentary public alarm. Politicians had become adept at muffling the clamour, whose volume faded as the racket of protective batteries increased.

As far back as September 1914 the airship shed at Düsseldorf had been bombed by the RNAS. By December Cologne and Friedrichshaven had received similar treatment. Towards Christmas the French damaged Freiburg railway station, and on May 26, 1915, dropped 87 bombs on the poison gas factory at Ludwigshaven. The following year Italian Capronis raided Ljubljana in the Balkans.

These missions showed what aeroplanes could achieve, as did the Germans' destruction of 8000 tons of Allied ammunition in a dump near St Omer on the night of July 20, 1916. But only on special occasions. The combination of careful planning, organisation, skill, and determination needed for operations of this type was not readily available.

Long-range assault had not lacked supporters. In mid-1916 Trenchard had asked for 10 squadrons of strategic machines, but with the proviso that 56 other squadrons first be supplied for immediate work on the Western Front. As usual the factories could not meet even his tactical needs.

Only the Navy responded in practical fashion, by establishing No. 3 Wing at Luxeuil-les-Bains in the Vosges. After an initial foray to the benzine store and barracks at the Mülheim near Freiburg the Sopwith 1½ Strutters joined French bombers in a force of 62 which set off for the Mauser Works at Oberndorf, a round trip of 223 miles, on October 12, 1916.

Bombs with a total weight of 8000 lb left the racks but on the return journey the machines were shot up by early Home Defence units, whose pilots included the embryo stars *Leutnant* Otto Kissenberth, *Leut* Hans Auer, *Vizfeldwebel* (Acting Sgt) Ludwig Hanstein, and *Vfw* (later General) Ernst Udet. Twenty-one crewmen were lost and undoubtedly casualties would have been worse but for the intervention of Nieuport scouts of the volunteer *Escadrille Americaine,* whose Raoul Lufbery became an official ace, his fifth victory being an Aviatick broken up by his bullets.

This ambitious operation, which killed or wounded 10 civilians and blew holes in some cottages, failed to interrupt Mauser's gun output. But it did highlight the problems confronting commanders of strategic bombing groups.

Before course was set technical defects stopped several machines from crossing the Lines. Cloud prevented others finding their place in the pattern. Bomb-sights were inadequate and ragged formation flying dispersed the load over a wide area.

Fighter escort was essential, in and out. But the scouts could not carry enough petrol. At the Rhine the Nieuports had been forced to return to Luxeuil for fuel, again picking up the bombers on their final lap.

Trying to land at dusk the American squadron's much-loved Norman Prince had died after catching his undercarriage on unseen high-tension wires. Clearly, lack of well-sited aerodromes and strong landing lights meant autumn and winter bombers starting before 1 pm, and poor weather might make that impracticable.

Undaunted, 3 Wing and some antiquated French Breguet 5s tackled the ironworks and factories of Hagondange on October 23, and during November the blast-furnaces of Völklingen and St Ingbert. Mist, fog and snow confined the Navy men to their slush-spread aerodrome until January 23, 1917, when frost-bite afflicted several flyers making for the Brebach furnaces at Saarbrücken.

Only 16 out of 24 machines reached the target and they were engaged by six Halberstadt scouts.

Two days later Brebach was on the board again, the target of 20 Sopwiths which drove off a few antique enemy aircraft—shortened officially to EA, but 'Huns' to the RFC whose humour was often inverted.

Newer types caught them in the Saar Valley during the Brebach mission of March 4, a fast Roland scout falling to Sopwith 9410, piloted by Flight Sub-Lieut Patteson, and gunlayer H. J. L. 'Bert' Hinkler—who 10 years on would set up a record by flying solo from England to Australia in 14½ days.

With the arrival of better equipment in the shape of twin-engined Handley Page bombers the Wing might have developed into a regular strategic force, but during Bloody April, when the Royal Flying Corps was ravaged by a *Luftstreitkräfte* (German Imperial Air Service) at the height of its power, it was disbanded to provide pilots for scout units required by Trenchard. Freiburg workers saw the last bombs tumble towards them on April 14.

So the Navy's valiant endeavour to break away from a 'support' role amounted to exploratory probes.

Thereafter Allied countries were to accomplish no more, their 'strategic' missions developing as extensions of the tactical offensive and designed to relieve immediate pressures on the armies. The Germans' own campaign was upset by High Command indecision and regal and political diffidence.

By July 1917 the British, already veterans of the Zeppelins and coastal shelling or both, were in low spirits. Casualty lists filled whole pages in newspapers as the Battles of Arras and Bapaume were followed rapidly by the Battles of Messines and Third Ypres. The U-boats' submarine harvest was scything food stocks. Retail prices had risen by 102 per cent, 37 per cent more than the cost-of-living index, restaurants rationed potatoes and meat, stores could not sell baked pastry, while rice, peas, and beans were also controlled. Shopping queues were part of the street scene.

Besides speeding the transfer of enemy Eastern Front troops to Flanders the breeze from fleeing Russian soldiers had swept across the White Cliffs of Dover. It fanned smouldering resentments over the soaring prices, unequal food distribution, restrictions on liquor and movement of labour, and the call-up of

100,000 young semi-skilled men hitherto exempt. Strikes, sometimes sparked by representatives of the International Workers of the World, a subversive American movement, crippled engineering and munitions plants in 48 towns, involved 200,000 employees, and cost Britain 1,500,000 working days.

Ramsay MacDonald, the Socialist leader, called a convention at Leeds 'to hail the Russian Revolution and to organise the British Democracy to follow Russia'. One aim was to form Workmen's and Soldiers' Councils in every urban and rural district. If this declaration constituted treason wily Prime Minister Lloyd George evidently decided it did not qualify woolly MacDonald for martyrdom. Instead he authorised an enquiry into industrial unrest, which dutifully discovered that the majority of working men were sensible of the national difficulties and had no intention of unfurling the Red Flag.

That, of course, was before Londoners became, as Lloyd George noted, 'stricken with nervous fear by the throbbing sound of German aeroplanes . . .' At that time it seemed likely the Gothas would penetrate other virtually 'open' (undefended) cities where panic would serve the disciples of dissatisfaction. With the July 7 invasion the Premier knew he would again have to face public and Parliamentary outbursts like those which had followed an attack on June 13, when with 162 killed and 432 injured the casualty list amounted to 75 per cent of that run up in 23 Zeppelin raids. Two fighter squadrons hastily transferred to Home Defence had been returned to France only a few hours before the second visitation, a fact rued by Sir David Henderson, Director of Military Aviation, as he surveyed the impertinent Gothas from a balcony of RFC HQ at the Hotel Cecil.

While rubble was being swept up journalists shied a few bricks of their own. The Press Association said the 'hostile air fleet presented an unbelievable spectacle as in stately procession it moved slowly, almost symmetrically spaced . . . daringly low . . .'

The *Sunday Pictorial*, so overcome by the 'poised kestrels' and 'air hawks' that it finally called them Taubes, was correct when it observed 'they hovered over London in a way which suggested they were seeking some particular prey—some particular spot on which to drop their bombs'.

*The Times* found the raid had produced 'much anger in the public mind', the aeroplanes' advent being heralded only 'by a large number of warnings privately given, though by no general warning'. It added a most telling point: 'Many people'—and this was not a leader writer's generalisation—'consider that one great defect in the present system is that the air defences are under the dual control of the Army and Navy.'

Fleet Street's spirited if belated assessment of the Gothas' success was summed up by the *Daily Mail*. Not since the Dutch Navy had ravaged the Medway in 1667 had Britain been so humiliated and disgraced. There was not a single redeeming feature and the Editor, the great Thomas Marlowe, blamed the Admiralty, the Horse Guards, and Air Service commands who were 'so heavily involved, and the position so grave, that the men who have failed should at once be called upon to resign and be replaced by young, more active, more energetic, minds'.

Simultaneously the War Cabinet met; in such gloom that a participant declared 'one would have thought the whole world was coming to an end'.

Lloyd George visited the East End to comfort the homeless; but even his Welsh rhetoric could not forestall the night-time smashing and looting of Hackney shops bearing German names, mob savagery which spread to the quiet suburbs of Tottenham and Highgate.

Militarily, his duty was clear. He must not undermine the Ypres 'push' by pulling out several squadrons for the protection of London. Politically, the civilian clamour must be quieted; and inevitably a thought occurred: Would the voters face the new dangers if they believed German families were suffering equally? That was when the signal went to Trenchard.

And it asked too much. For the most part crews of single-engined machines would have to fly double the distance covered by England-raiding Gothas, with no reference points to compare with two coastlines, across mountainous terrain, and within reach of the enemy's hardened front-line fighters. To be effective they would have to do this without respite, somehow avoiding losses of more than a few per cent in men or material, somehow attaining unheard-of accuracy in placing their explosives.

Trenchard saw further than this. He declared that strategic bombing might bring with it the attempted destruction of open towns, for 'unless we are determined and prepared to go one better than the Germans, whatever they may do and whether their reply is in the air or against our prisoners or otherwise, it will be infinitely better not to attempt reprisals at all'.

The Prime Minister sought the politician's infalliable remedy, a committee, this time on 'Air Organisation and Home Defence Against Air Raids' and headed by the flamboyant South African general Jan Christian Smuts. Fortunately for aeronautical progress Smuts' principal adviser, and the true father of the Royal Air Force, was the mild-mannered but erudite and highly perceptive Sir David Henderson.

While the Committee sifted evidence and wrote its 6000-word report Trenchard—with the unstinted co-operation of Paul-Fernand du Peuty, French air commander and an old friend—was surveying sites for strategic aerodromes in the Departements de Meurthe-et-Moselle and Vosges, east of Paris and on the verge of Germany proper.

These fields were deplorable. Stony moor or marsh, they were walled by hills and woods whose sole benefit lay in their camouflaging character. Level places were hard to find and these were corrugated by furrows up to 3 ft 6 in. deep. One of the best, and among Trenchard's early acquisitions, was Tantonville, beside a village famed—at least by the French—for its beer, an L-shaped expanse with a wood in the angle of the letter. The landing area was soft, sloped, and spread in the shadow of high-voltage wires.

Obviously months of labour by Indian and Cochin Chinese pioneer gangs lay ahead before even a few sites could accept heavily laden and, comparatively speaking, speedy aircraft with any degree of safety. Draining and levelling and the laying of approach roads were immediate priorities; but installation of internal electric power for lighting, workshops, and fuel stores was also important. Room was scarce, many ground staff having to be billeted in villages two or more miles away. Although Nancy and Toul were within range of a squadron tender petrol could ill be spared and therefore amusements would be of the simplest.

Nothing in the prospect pleased either stern leader or sensitive man in the chemistry of Trenchard. Nor, as August ended, did he welcome Smuts' suggestions for formation of an air organisation separate from the War Office and Admiralty—a move which, in wartime, he believed could disturb the fragile harmony cultivated by the Services. Nearly 50 years ahead of his time, he preferred a Defence Ministry incorporating 'offices' of the three arms.

The paragraph which was to concern him directly ran:

'While our Western Front may be moving forward at a snail's pace in Belgium and France the air battle in 1918 will be far behind the Rhine . . . Its continuous and intense pressure against the chief industrial centres of the enemy as well as on his lines of communication may form the determining factor in bringing about the peace.' The surplus of engines and machines being built should have regard to the strategical purpose to which they were going to be put.

This stemmed from Smuts' confidence that aircraft production in the 12 months ahead would outstrip Army and Navy needs: and in September the War Cabinet gave panicky endorsement to the recommendations after a series of Zeppelin and Gotha sorties over English factories.

To Field Marshal Haig went the October 1 signal—'Cabinet desires immediate action against those German objectives which can be reached from neighbourhood of Nancy. Send Trenchard to discuss scale . . .' The following afternoon Trenchard told the PM that six days after the first aeroplanes arrived at Ochey, a peacetime French aerodrome he was borrowing, and from which RNAS machines had once flown, they would be in action.

The operations, he asserted, would not fail but their degree of effectiveness would be limited by the smallness of the force, its lack of long-range experience, and the weather. So at the outset he pronounced the history of the independent bombers, a prophecy never to be contradicted.

His own unease was echoed by Smuts, who confessed that he now knew the surplus of 3000 aeroplanes on which he had based his establishment of an Air Ministry was false. The chasm between Government expectations and production figures was an old bogey to the aviator, still awaiting bombers 'granted' him in 1916.

Once more he was being committed to a desperate enterprise without proper preparation; this time even denied the blessing of Haig, who rejected outright the idea that any of 'his' flyers should be removed from his jurisdiction.

But the die was cast and Trenchard had picked his croupier. Cyril Newall (later Marshal of the Royal Air Force Lord Newall), son of a soldier, had been one of the Indian Army officers chosen in 1913 for flying instruction. Throughout Bloody April he had been Trenchard's commander of 9th (HQ) Wing, where at the age of 31 his steadiness, technical knowledge, and ingenuity were remarkable even under wartime stimulus. Destined to be an architect of British fighter readiness in World War

II, he was now articulate about future co-operation with Allies, especially the Americans—one of whom, Olive Tennyson Foster of Boston, he would marry.

His new command was the specially created 41st Wing, whose headquarters he established at Bainville-sur-Madon on October 11. On that day, too, five of his aeroplanes reached Ochey.

These were De Havilland 4 two-seaters of 55 Sqn, which had been blooded for seven months in tactical bombing, photo reconnaissance, and close-formation combat. The machines were sturdy, fast, manœuvrable, and comfortable, their only defect being the four feet of petrol tank between pilot and observer which prevented communication except over crude speaking tubes. They arrived with Western Front symbols, a white triangle on the fuselage. Entering into the spirit of their pioneer role the Squadron substituted a winged figure dropping a bomb on factories. But Newall, determined to give German Intelligence no clues, ruled that all his units should be anonymous.

In its drab olive-green and grey Fours 55 Sqn (CO, Major J. E. A. 'Jack' Baldwin, later Air Marshal Sir John), probably the best day-bombardment outfit of all time, would set a standard of efficiency, integrity, and valour unsurpassed by any Service unit.

As companions it had 100 Sqn (Major M. G. Christie), whose lattice-tailed FE 2bs began organised raiding by starlight the previous April, and A (Naval) Sqn under Sqn Cmdr K. S. Savory, some of whose Handley Page o/100s had been pulled off inshore anti-submarine patrols from Redcar, North Yorkshire. Kenneth Savory was the only officer with very long-distance time. In June he had flown an o/100 2000 miles from England to Lemnos in the Aegean Sea, by way of Paris, Rome, and the Balkans. Above the Albanian Alps at 10,000 ft water froze in the radiators.

It was a pathetically small Wing, although inured to the long-distance bombing practice of the time; that is, flights of up to 100 miles across low-lying country, undertaken when weather prospects were reasonably good, and not too far from the help of roving scouts. Bad-weather flying had fallen mainly to artillery co-operation squadrons working near the ground and within a few miles of a landing ground.

Nevertheless, on October 15, when Andrew Bonar Law, Deputy Prime Minister of the Coalition Government, told Members that an Air Ministry would be set up it became obvious that some time 41st Wing would cease to be an ill-kept sideshow. Indeed, 55 Sqn was now assured of replacement aircraft, consequent on the reassignment of 50 intended for the collapsed Russian Front.

Newall set his eastern limit of attack on a line Cologne–Frankfurt–Stuttgart, roughly 125 miles from the trench line on an arc to the front of Ochey. Although optimistic in that season, the target area was a vital industrial one and well within the fuel range of the HPs and DH 4s, provided the former did not lose the way and the others were not driven off course by interceptors. The FEs could be employed only on shorter missions.

On his map were the coal and iron fields of Lorraine and the Saar, chemical works at Mannheim and Oppau, and factories for aircraft engines and magnetos, locomotives and submarine components. Blast-furnaces were splendid pinpoints, if not so sensitive as power stations. And Germany was relying on Lorraine and Luxembourg for about 80 per cent of her iron-ore supplies, 20 to 25 per cent of which was smelted locally.

Railway systems were also priority marks. French Intelligence had calculated that every day 10,600 trucks of 15 tons each went through the junctions of Metz-Sablons, Metz-Woippy, Conflans-Lonquyon, Athus-Pattingen, Thionville, and Bettenbourg, all stations on the periphery of the iron basins. They were taking ore to works on the right bank of the Moselle, to Westphalia, and to the Rhine. Or returning for loads. So the produce of collieries, awkward objectives, could be destroyed by a few well-aimed bombs. In fact this was preferable to assailing the mines directly, as it wasted the labour of thousands of colliers, wrecked trains together with cargoes, and tore up the tracks along which front-line reinforcements also travelled.

The Wing's first mission, however, was to the heart of the coal district—Saarbrücken, a round trip of 100 miles. Two flights of 55 Sqn, led by Capts J. M. Burd and W. B. Farrington, loosed 1792 lb of bombs on the Burbach plant with what the French journals next day described as '*beaucoup de succes*', killing five, injuring nine, and causing just £850 worth of damage. Trenchard's 'six days' forecast had been right.

The next few days were unfit for any bird but a penguin, but on October 21 the squadron met its first opposition when dumping 2464 lb of explosive on a factory at Bous, WNW of Saarbrücken. A DH 4 fell to a German scout, the crew becoming prisoners.

While this raid was taking place Winston S. Churchill, Minister of Munitions, approved the Wing's principles and, in a paper outlining prospects for 1918, warned of the futility of indiscriminate bombing. 'It is not reasonable to speak of an air offensive as if it were going to finish the war by itself', he wrote. 'It is improbable that any terrorisation of the civil population which could be achieved by air attack would compel the Government of a great nation to surrender.

'Familiarity with bombardment, a good system of dugouts or shelters, a strong control of police and military authorities, should be sufficient to preserve the national fighting power unimpaired . . . Nothing that we have learned of the capacity of the German population to endure suffering justifies us in assuming that they could be cowed into submission by such methods, or, indeed, that they would not be rendered more desperately resolved by them.

'Therefore our air offensive should consistently be directed at striking at the bases and communications upon whose structure the fighting power of his armies and his fleets of the sea and of the air depends. Any injury which comes to the civil population from this process of attack must be regarded as incidental and inevitable.'

Despite his fervent agreement with these convictions, Newall cannot have found them easy to implement when the visibility before his pilots varied from murky to opaque.

His main navigational aid was a series of 'lighthouses', automatic shutter lamps flashing Morse numbers or letters, detectable at 2000 ft, and sited in a half-circle forward of the aerodrome. They were to prove a godsend to tired crews in limping aeroplanes on the inward journey.

Nine £10,000 Handley Pages were prepared by Naval A on the 24th and three had set course for Saarbrücken before heavy rain caused Savory to 'scrub' the operation. The last machine had Flight Sub-Lieut Geoffrey Linnell of Wilby, Northants, at the control wheel. Heading past Lighthouse Z, Ochey's own beacon, he noted A and D 19 kilometres to east and west and held the nose between them for Nancy, which he skirted as the first chill drops rapped his windshield and damped the bright blink of Lighthouse B. Twisting round he stared through the inverted V of the stout centre-section strut along the canvas fuselage to the square rear cockpit, where his gunner huddled miserably between two Lewis guns on candlestick mountings, isolated but for the continuous cable carrying messages in empty Very cases. The rain was now splashing off the observer's deserted seat beside him and the Scarff gun ring around the front bomb-aiming 'office'. Squinting past the screen Linnell could hardly discern Lighthouse C, his final guide and three miles from the Lines.

Folding the pulpy map he pushed on grimly across the frontier town of Château-Salins, his only illumination coming from the greenish aura of the instrument bulbs and the fiery glow from the exhausts of the Rolls-Royce engines as they whirled their 11 ft propellers behind his ears. After an age he picked out distant splodges of light that denoted a Saarbrücken unaccustomed to nocturnal visitations. As he did so an engine missed a beat, spluttered, shuddered, died.

Cursing, Linnell heaved the HP round, his stomach sinking with the thought of the impossible distance to home. By now the rain, borne on a 40 mph wind, was turning to sleet and snow and he was flying blind, dependent on air speed indicator and compass. Dimly he noticed red sparks beyond his wingtips, but an isolated *flakartillarie* (anti-aircraft) battery was not to be his downfall.

With full power the HP was pleasant to pilot although in gusty weather her lateral stability was suspect and muscle was needed to make her level up. Linnell, one leg knotted on the rudder bar to counteract the pull of his sound engine, had lost too much height and suddenly saw the looming shadow of a hill.

As he heaved on the wheel the dazzling snake of a *scheinwerfer* (searchlight)—co-operating with 10·5 cm guns on the Saar range—lashed at him.

Blinded, he yanked the nose too far, lost flying speed, and tumbled into a spin. The hill rushed up and snatched the HP's long top-wing extension . . .

When the crashing stopped Linnell crawled to the rear and pulled out his unconscious gunner. Everyone was safe, but a few hours later Savory had to report the loss of two Handleys.

It was not surprising that Linnell had seen nothing of other aeroplanes, all of which had taken off individually, but 12 from 100 Sqn were airborne in the vicinity. They were quaint craft these FE 2bs, fighters in 1916 and now the only operational British 'pushers', with their crews crouched before the engine and the propeller revolving between naked booms leading to the tail unit. The bomber version had a tough V-undercarriage but in a bad landing the 'Fee' was likely to somersault, caterpulting the observer and pinning the pilot. Although slow, it was stable and could carry on wing racks a variety of loads.

The least elegant of Newall's marauders these Fees certainly were, but their flyers were fresh from mayhem after dark on the Western Front where besides strafing aerodromes they had 'busted' trains and road transport with one-pounder pom-poms. Buoyed by these experiences they reached the rail tracks on the way to Saarbrücken and let go twelve 230 lb and twenty-three 25 lb bombs over stations and goods sidings. One heavy bomb knocked a locomotive off Wallerburg crossover and others reduced carriages of a train in Homburg station to matchwood.

Needled by sleet, conscious of their choking engines, the pilots groped back to Ochey. In turn they fired Very cartridges as a recognition signal or Morsed their letter with undercarriage lights. For the benefit of ground defences searchlights held on their blue-white-red tail fins as they swung into the flare path of blazing petrol cans—some airfields had electric bulbs placed on three-feet-high stakes—30 yards apart. After a run of 200 yards the pilots, warned by a red lamp, closed their throttles and rumbled off to their hangars.

All except two. Forced down midway, Lieut W. H. Jones of Swansea (observer, Lieut R. S. Greenslade of Somerset) and Lieut L. M. Archibald of Toronto (Lieut J. S. Godard of Ottawa), became prisoners and 100's first casualties in 39 strategic missions with FE 2bs.

Both components of Newall's force now understood the nature of their jobs and for the rest of the month they built up flying time with minor raids on Saarbrücken, Völklingen, and Pirmasens, and on Kaiserslautern, where German interceptors made six DH 4s waste their bombs but at last lost one of their number to the Wing. Weather continued poor and this, combined with 55's move to Tantonville, allowed only one operation in November. It was not a promising augury.

Trenchard, automatically halving a Government figure, thought he would be extremely lucky to receive 20 out of 40 promised bomber squadrons by the end of 1918. Nor was he confident about a new type, the DH 9, because 90 per cent of cylinder blocks necessary for its power plant, the Siddeley Puma, were defective. On November 16 he told Major-General John M. Salmond, Director General of Military Aeronautics, that the Nine would have a poorer performance than the Four and would not reach 15,000 ft when war-loaded. He deemed the situation 'critical'.

Nine days later he wrote: 'I want to bomb Germany, but please remember that if we lose half our machines doing so, the good morale effect which is three-quarters of the work will be on the German side and not ours. I am in no way trying to upset the policy of the War Cabinet for bombing Germany with a large number of machines. What I am trying to do is to do it efficiently, and the crux of the whole matter seems to be whether we are going to have efficient machines to do it with.'

The Air Board, almost at the end of its life, heard him explain on November 25 that the DH 9s should be regarded as a New Year stop-gap. Were he committed to large numbers the casualties would jeopardise the continuation, let alone the extension, of long-distance day bombing. He snorted at an official report forecasting that 5000 fighting planes fitted with American Liberty engines would be in France by July. (Fewer than 500 were so equipped at the Armistice.)

Within three weeks Trenchard's strictures had been conveniently forgotten. Fifty-seven magical words stilled the winds, dispersed the clouds, multiplied men and machines, and vanished the task.

They were trumpeted on December 14 by Lord Rothermere, a commercial man in, but not of, Fleet Street and head of the Air Board, in a stirring atmosphere of blood-red Burgundy and cigar smoke conjured up by the Gray's Inn Benchers to honour something they described, with unwonted legal inaccuracy, as 'The Air Service'.

To rapturous cheers he exclaimed: 'At the Air Board we are wholeheartedly in favour of air reprisals! It is our duty to avenge the murder of innocent women and children. As the enemy elects, so it will be the case of "eye for an eye, a tooth for a tooth", and in this respect we shall slave for complete and satisfying retaliation.'

It was as though the Lords of the Admiralty had 'requested and required' a commodore with a battleship, a cruiser, and a gunboat—equivalents of the Wing's squadrons—to reduce Germany by deliberately bombarding homesteads. 'Women and children first' in reverse . . .

For an age still clinging to its rags of chivalry the doctrine was morally sickening. In practical terms it was a non-starter by Wilful Ignorance out of Sentimentality. Trenchard turned his back on the exhortation. And soon there came a sign that the 41st Wing was making the Germans apprehensive.

In December 55 Sqn made further deliveries at the Burbach works and Pirmasens; and their activity was the catalyst for several attempts by German bombers to strafe Ochey.

Christmas Eve was the Wing's best day. Led by Captains Farrington and Stevens 12 Fours left for a chlorine gas and chemical factory, the Badische Anilin and Soda Fabrik, at Mannheim. This city, at the junctions of the Rivers Rhine and Neckar and the chief centre of trade on the Upper Rhine, also manufactured machinery and glass, and weather had frustrated several previous attempts to make the 200-mile trip.

Two machines returned with engine trouble but the rest jettisoned uniformly from 13,000 ft. *Flak* was fierce and accurate, 26 guns sowing the sky with acrid black cauliflowers from the eastern slopes of the Vosges mountains. One holed Four dropped, but as they went sixteen bombs slithered down on the main station, into the Lanz works, at Ludwigshaven across the river, and around the munitions factory between Mudenheim and Rheingonheim.

The AA fire—which had also wounded an observer—died out, to let 11 scouts into the ring. Five actually gained the Fours' height but contented themselves with squirting from twin synchronised Maxim guns at a safe distance. The cold was intense, 10 degrees Fahrenheit at ground level, and mist gathering over landmarks in the Palatinate was a more obstinate opponent for the fast bombers as they drew away.

A few days later the *Daily Express* correspondent in Geneva told 55 Sqn how closely they had come to removing the All Highest. His report ran:

'. . . the Kaiser and his Staff had an extremely narrow escape. They were returning from the Verdun Front on their way to Berlin and the Imperial train passed through Mannheim station a bare hour before the structure was partially wrecked . . .

'The train was, in fact, the last to leave Mannheim and none has arrived since at Bâle from that point. The permanent way has been destroyed for some distance beyond the station, thus cutting connection with the north.

'Two bombs fell on the Palace of the Palatinate and one on the suspension bridge which crosses the Neckar. Both structures were badly damaged. A munitions factory in a northern suburb of the town was blown up but as most of the workers were on holiday there were few casualties. A number of people were killed or injured in the town.'

With this raid the German Press began its outcry against the wickedness of bombing 'harmless open towns'. Four days later the Wing acquired greater status and another title—VIII Brigade.

# 2 *'... the heaven was black with clouds, and there was a great rain.' (1 Kings 18:45)*

This was the winter of British discontent. A low blow had knocked Russia out of the arena; following the loss of 600,000 troops at Caporetto, Italy was reeling on the ropes; France huddled exhausted in a corner; and America was still in the changing room. Haig was fighting the Frenchman's war to the last Englishman. The RFC's ground-strafing 'shows' were once more raising the Western Front squadrons' casualty rate to 30 per cent, and Trenchard was sucked into the politicians' maw.

Lord Rothermere had been appointed Air Minister and, as part of a plot to discomfit Haig—whose Government stock had shrunk alarmingly with the slaughter of Third Ypres, commonly called Passchendaele—pressed Trenchard into an Hotel Cecil chair as Chief of Air Staff.

In a Ritz suite at 3.30 am, after 12 hours of threats and promises, Rothermere and Lord Northcliffe, his Press baron brother, played the ace of clubs. If, they said, Trenchard did not accept the post they would exploit his retention on the Western Front by Haig—who 'did not know how to use the air'—to belabour the GOC even more.

Despite all his previous encounters with the breed, Trenchard could not circumvent the slipperiness of political animals, but beside theirs his vision was telescopic. Before leaving his flyers with Haig's grudging consent, he half persuaded the French, whose aviation was now represented by General M. Duval, that a British-controlled strategic offensive would benefit their Army when it could be re-established for a major offensive.

His arrangements with the Americans better displayed his selflessness and insight into the destiny of aeronautics. His principal contact was Brigadier-General B. D. Foulois, who had been taught to 'solo' in three hours by the Wright Brothers at College Park, Maryland, and now commanded the Aviation Section of the Signal Corps in Europe. But nobody on the Continent was so valuable a supporter of Trenchard's concept as was an impatient, outspoken, extrovert major in charge of tactical air support for the American Expeditionary Force.

William Mitchell, born in Nice of Scottish-American parents, was 38 in May 1917 when he first made Trenchard welcome his resourceful mind and hustling manner. He in turn was inspired by the theories of this strange, booming, introvert whom he described as 'one of the greatest figures in the whole European contest'. For this faith he would suffer worse than Trenchard. The US Army and Navy had no use in peacetime for air-minded officers who demonstrated that capital ships could be sunk by aeroplanes and prophesied, 18 years ahead of reality, that the Japanese would make a 'sneak' raid on American territory. They court-martialled him for speaking out of turn.

Just now, however, life was fun. Dolled up in fur-trimmed British Warm and pink trousers he could contour-chase in a Spad 13 fighter, spying the land and dreaming of assaults by Handley Page loads of airborne infantry. Though his pilots reckoned him too old for such larks, Foulois—if not Washington's Wingless Wonders sent to the Staff 'over there'—listened to his radical ideas and trusted his enthusiasm for Trenchard's.

As a consequence of this goodwill and his own diplomatic approach Trenchard could lay the foundations of a multi-nation air fleet which he considered would be invincible by 1920.

Supposing the armies remained stalemated and the Fatherland obviated the Royal Navy blockade, that force could lay waste to every important German city within three years. His scheme envisaged American aviators and ground personnel coming under his flag for strategic work so long as the British were the 'predominant partner'. Promotion within the force would be on merit irrespective of nationality. When the US strength—202 combat squadrons were proposed for July 1919—overtook that of the Royal Air Force Trenchard would automatically hand over his command.

In his staccato fashion Trenchard reported the tentative agreement to Rothermere: 'I feel certain that this will be the best way to run it . . . I am certain by the way the Americans talked to me that they will do it. This means no delay in our arrangements . . . The only question is whether the machines will be efficient. I can assure you the organisation will be.'

So he crossed the grey Channel and though no trumpets sounded for him on the other side a knighthood arrived with the New Year's Honours.

While Major-General Salmond (later Sir John, Marshal of the Royal Air Force), an expert in Army co-operation, settled into Trenchard's old job, the editor of *Flight*, the much respected aviation journal, expressed the new sense of retaliation pervading military circles. On January 3 he wrote: '. . . we have almost come to accept Lord Rothermere's code of revenge, and to place our policy of counter raids on no higher plane than that of avenging the murders of our defenceless citizens. But we think the matter goes beyond that. In the first place, the duty is laid upon our authorities of defending our shores, and if that can only be done—as we believe to be the case—by raiding the enemy's towns from the air until he cries for mercy, then let us raid them as often and as heavily as need be.

'We shall in the course of these raids undoubtedly kill and injure German civilians. We regret that necessity, but we cannot get away from the fact that the necessity has been forced upon us by the prior action of an enemy who has adopted frightfulness as his creed in the belief that he was the only one with a stomach for it. It has taken us long enough to learn that lesson, but we have learnt it now, and all we have to say is "let there be raids!" '

Newall wished the shocking weather—sleet, snow, mist—would let him oblige.

Layers of silk, wool, and leather swathing the crews until they resembled brown grubs might serve for a couple of hours over the Front but flights of double and treble that length needed something more efficient. Flyers who resorted to the Edwardian schoolboy's 'winter warmer'—a tin stuffed with smouldering rags—eventually found their thighs blistering before they could unfasten jackets and sheepskin thigh boots and reach the overheated containers.

Electrical kit with wires strung on a vest, through gloves, and attached to a powerpack was available but without guarantee. When a machine dived the system generated too much electricity and finger burns became common. Extra body wrappings might restrict a pilot's movements but he considered them preferable to a heating apparatus which burned up or faded on him at the slip of a terminal.

In the first fortnight of 1918 the new Brigade's progress was disheartening, only 16 out of 28 machines from 100 Sqn reaching two near targets, Maizieres and Conflans. Bomb flashes were seen in the murk below but their message could not be deciphered. One HP from Naval A aimed for Thionville, called Diedenhofen by the Germans, and finally terminated its wanderings at Courcelles, where the bomb aimer was frustrated by a carpet of mist.

On the 14th 55 Sqn, whose CO was now Major Alexander Gray, later Air Vice-Marshal, awoke to clearer skies and 12 DH 4s visited Karlsruhe, where they dropped a ton of bombs, including phosphorus, on to railway shops and a cadet school. Pictures showed dense white smoke spreading across the town from blazing tobacco trucks. Opposition was slight although some observers had added a second Lewis gun to their Scarff mounting, increasing fire at the expense of mobility.

Good fortune also attended the Fees that night over Thionville steel works where a 230-pounder and a sprinkling of Coopers put paid to an AA battery. Other bombers closed a main railway line for two days. Engine trouble and high winds upset several other raids; and violent and well-directed *flak* greeted an HP of Naval A—redesignated 16(Naval)—near Arnaville railway bridge.

This was the first experience of orderly anti-aircraft defence, which thereafter would menace night flyers along every lane into the German hinterland. Always lagging slightly behind the impetus of the assault, if its bark rarely deterred its bite steadily bled Newall of his small reserves of strength.

Fledgling crews quickly learned to read the AA signs. Soundless white puffs or, on a pitch-black night, red fireflies, meant the shells were bursting at a safe distance; a muffled 'whooof!' with a red blink had to be countered by a height or course adjustment; a brilliant flash and a sharp 'craaak!' and the machine was in danger from splinters. Real trouble came with the stench of burnt cordite and the 'click-click' of hits on spars or the drumming of rent fabric.

Apart from sound detection—the Allies alone used listening trumpets—the Fatherland was exploiting every method of resistance, the most bizarre being a barrage of balloons. In fine weather *drachen* (dragon) balloons with 80 cubic metres capacity and a single tail stabiliser were sent up. In rough conditions these were replaced by rows of small spheres. Either type dangled steel cables about two inches thick from maximum heights of between 5000 and 7200 ft. The wires were usually single but could be cross-connected by shorter lengths arranged as an apron. Barrages were 300 or 400 yards apart, but drawn tighter around the objective.

They covered six danger areas. Forty-nine balloons were at 2500 ft on the line Hayange–Knutange–Algrange; 50 at 7200 ft, Leverkusen-Manfort; 62 at 300 ft, Rombach-Hagondange-Maizieres; 30 with electrified cables, Ludwigshaven-Mannheim. Works directors were not impressed by them, partly because they were expected to contribute to the cost, which rose as high as £150,000. Only at Saarbrücken, where 249 balloons with aprons were arranged in two layers several hundred feet apart, did the population feel the scheme was effective.

In the Esch basin 35 balloons were ready but seldom run out, and when in the 5 pm gloom of January 24 ten Fees rumbled on a 200-mile round trip to Trier (Trèves to the French), a Prussian and ancient Roman city south-west of Coblenz, their pilots were concerned only that the wind should not change.

Coming up to the environs they watched the lights flick out and *flak* start around the Central Station. Boring in, the FEs smacked eight 230 lb, twenty-two 112 lb, eighteen 25 lb bombs, and the incendiaries on to the steel works and town but without being able to classify results.

An FE numbered A 852 went low, Lieut F. E. le Fevre, MC, of Sutton (Surrey) pumping bullets from the observer's Lewis, and lurched as AA lead slashed the rudder controls. Second Lieut Louis G. Taylor of Upper Tooting tried to steer south but skidded south-west, travelling like this for 30 miles until he came to Esch in Luxembourg. Before he could evade it the 4000 ft balloon barrage reared before them.

Le Fevre rattled at a *drachen*, but to no effect, and the Fee would not climb. Sweating in the cold, the pilot wriggled his lopsided machine into a clear space and underneath a string of 'sausages'. At the moment he eased the stick the Fee bucked—and started backwards. On the verge of a stall Taylor stuffed down the nose with the ASI stuck at 30 mph. The ailerons failed, and it dawned frighteningly on the occupants of the shallow nacelle that they were wrapped in the net. The pilot was separated from space by his waist strap, the observer by his angled legs and grip on the Lewis mounting.

For five interminable minutes Taylor gingerly tried to dive, hoping the Fee's momentum and weight would drag the tentacles to the ground and snap them. The first part he managed, but the aeroplane also sank until a quarry, topped by a clump of trees, lay in its path. Taylor hauled back the stick and the Fee tipped on to a wing which crunched against the field just beyond the crater's rim. Like a cork from a bottle Le Fevre popped over the Lewis. Dazed by a blow from the engine, Taylor hung from the cockpit, a wing wagging above him, until his observer called, 'All right, old thing, out you come,' and helped him down.

For a few minutes they wandered aimlessly, being brought out of their shock by the flash of a rifle 20 yards away. Before they could move 10 German soldiers, interspersing their bellowing with shots, burst through the foliage. The flyers hugged the ground as the slugs flew wildly. They looked up at a ring of knee-boots and were pushed to the guardhouse.

In the crude hut the questions began—'What is your plane? Where have you been? How many bombs were carried? How much petrol?' And, shivering but resolute, they replied as aggressively as possible—that being Intelligence advice on how to deflate German guards—with their ranks, names, and numbers.

At 9.30 pm they were driven to Esch and in the car heard a 100 Sqn machine droning homewards. The following day a staff car returned them to the scene of their misfortune. Taylor sat by the guardhouse, on a wire drum which controlled the balloon barrage. From it he inspected the Fee's remains.

Shrapnel had riddled the planes and nacelle which had been driven into the earth. A tail boom was severed near the main plane and the engine was perched on a chewed-up wing. A balloon cable was wrapped round another plane and it had missed the cockpits by two feet, knifing three-quarters of the way from leading to trailing edge of both top and bottom planes. Sawing backwards it had sliced the aileron balance wires and through the bomb carrier until halted by the heavier steel of the Michelin flare rack. The undercarriage had vanished and the tail, devoid of fabric, drooped lugubriously.

More questions, by a Gotha pilot, followed, plus a two-hour drive to Thionville where the guards used their rifle butts to beat away infuriated civilians clawing at the scared prisoners—a foretaste of the mindless anger to which most shot-down bomber crews would be subjected. The couple also had a mouthful of the

Royal Navy's blockade, greasy black bread and grey acorn coffee.

A jeering mob lined their passage to the railway station in the morning and they were thankful to reach Jarny. Here they received the psychological treatment of fragrant surroundings, pleasant interrogators, and sudden confrontation with the products of photo-reconnaissance. They were indeed taken aback by pictures, 'shot' from a Rumpler C-VII at 18,000 ft, of Ochey aerodrome; and by details of 'A' Squadron—the only information slightly out of date—and of their own 100, complete with COs' names. Taylor and Le Fevre said nothing, but Intelligence officers can glean much from an indrawn breath or a tightened cheek muscle.

There were many people interested in the first flyers downed by a balloon barrage and on the 26th they were transferred to neighbouring Conflans, where they witnessed a big ceremonial parade in honour of the Kaiser's birthday and were given a 'celebration' meal of soup, meat, potatoes, sauerkraut, and bread. The subsequent three days were spent in a POW cage, followed by a march back to Conflans. The cookless tour continued with a spell at the old castle of Montmédy—where a French-speaking German posed as a prisoner but failed to deceive the ravenous but alert young officers. Four days and 12 slices of bread passed before Intelligence smilingly gave up.

The couple were dismissed to the prisoners' hostel at Karlsruhe, where they were confined with RFC officers—whose hasty signs indicated the microphone concealed in the wall. That exhausted the tricks. With 300 others they spent the 'duration' in the town's official *Kriegsgefangenlager*.

When news of this unique German victory reached London the scientists produced slide-rules and tables. They had to devise a counter-measure, and although designer Geoffrey de Havilland was adamant that nobody could survive a deliberate collision with a balloon cable a test pilot named Roderic Hilll (later Air Chief Marshal Sir Roderic) insisted he might.

After several weeks of effort and errors an FE 2b sprouted a bowsprit, attached under the nacelle and protruding several feet. Wires splayed from it back to the interplane struts, and it was suggested that they would deflect any balloon cable into which a night bomber might run. Not until May 28, and after last-minute modifications when they shifted the wires to the wing-tips, was the machine considered aerodynamically safe. To watch

Hill, whose technical brilliance as well as courage were also being applied to the DH 9 trials, Royal Aircraft Factory experts Dr F. A. Lindemann (later Lord Cherwell) and Capt G. H. B. Dobson came to Martlesham Heath at 4.15 am. Doctors and fire crews stood by.

Wearing an asbestos suit, Hill climbed the Fee to 3000 ft and flew straight for the balloon, trailing its steel cable against the flushing dawn. He rammed at 55 mph, and a 12 ft blue streak of fire marked the impact. The cable skated easily along the fender wire and should have flipped off the end. But the tense onlookers saw the Fee check and shake; then, with the cable gnawing into the wing-tip, gyrate for two and a half turns before wrenching loose in a shower of fabric. It dropped steeply, a chunk of the top wing missing, yet Hill somehow juggled it into a landing. The feat earned him the Air Force Cross, one of four Royal Air Force decorations for devotion to duty which would be instituted in July.

The solution was only partial and was left that way. For despite the damage they could inflict balloon webs first had to catch their fly, and this they could not manage. Still, their presence was forbidding and kept many raiders at levels where bomb-sights were least efficient.

As February opened, VIII Brigade was formally constituted, with Newall's elevation and Baldwin's promotion to command of the 41st Wing, which would remain the only independent Wing until creation of the 83rd on July 1 and of the 88th on October 17.

It was not a distinguished month, rain, cloud, and engine trouble spoiling 13 missions undertaken with stamina and intelligence—55 Sqn, for instance, bringing back all their bombs when they were baulked by a thick layer over Mannheim.

So black were the nights that without the help of incendiaries most results could not be registered, a situation pertaining on February 9. Four Fee crews crossed the Lines at 3000 ft and at Lighthouse C set course NNW for Courcelles. Three of the Beardmores roared away happily at 1200 rpm, giving a speed of 70 mph. The other worried Lieut O. B. Swart of Germiston, South Africa, but 'being a new pilot I was ashamed to return'.

After 40 minutes the machines let down beside the railway junction, Lieut W. Edwardes-Evans, MC, of Manchester smashing a searchlight reflector with Lewis fire and the lead machine lighting up the target with phosphorus. The remainder toggled into the fire. Ground machine guns began a rapid tattoo, which encouraged Swart to turn north sharply and give his observer, Lieut A. Fielding-Clarke of Reading, his right of reply. Several tracers went into Courcelles station. By now the machines were scattering for home, one with a severed strut, and in opening the throttle to pursue them Swart lost several cylinders. He was then at 1900 ft with a strong west wind impeding him. Anxiously he switched on the gravity tank, but engine vibration became worse, revolutions tumbled.

Alerted by the spluttering, the light *flak* increased its 'hate', and the engine packed up. Searchlights jerked in pursuit of the gliding Fee and at 200 ft Swart abandoned his efforts to restart the Beardmore.

Releasing a parachute flare he also sparked the wing-tip lights and discovered a clearing to the east.

From a tight bank he touched down smoothly within 10 yards —among hundreds of hares 'sitting bolt upright with the gleam of the reflected light shining out of their great saucy eyes'.

Swart was not sure how densely the area was 'occupied' but had an idea that if he could find a telephone the French operator could connect him with friends. He had walked a hundred yards when a horse-cart overtook him. Bending down a German soldier in a fur cap challenged: '*Sind sie ein Franzosischer Flieger?*' Thinking quickly, the South African snapped in schoolboy German: 'No, don't you know who I am? Have you seen my automobile?' And stamped off angrily, away from the Fee in case the German followed.

After an interval he doubled back to Fielding-Clarke, but by shielded torchlight they failed to find the cause of the breakdown. Nothing was left but a walk-out, and they hacked the controls with a jack-knife and ripped the marked maps to shreds.

Still buoyant, the couple trudged off in their floppy, soft-soled flying boots—excruciating wear for long treks—and for the next few hours dodged enemy sentries and AA emplacements by spotting the red glow of cigars.

They decided to hole-up during the day and at dawn found a mud wallow which they camouflaged with branches. German troops passed them frequently and about noon they heard the purr of an aeroplane. Peeping through the foliage they discovered pamphlets pattering down or hooked on bushes around them. They were surprised, not by the propaganda droppings from the Adastral House 'factory' of Captain Chalmers Mitchell, but by the method of delivery. Since October 17, when 2nd Lieuts E. Scholtz and H. C. Wookey of 11 Sqn had been taken prisoner and sentenced to 10 years' penal servitude for scattering leaflets urging soldiers to desert, the British General Staff—in one of those squeamish moments not experienced by German generals —had allowed only miniature balloons to carry 'incitement literature' across the Lines.

More practical issues impinged on Swart and Fielding-Clarke. They could not play possum for much longer and the pilot cursed himself for not having brought a message-pigeon which might have summoned a pick-up machine or brought bombs on to neighbouring batteries. In whispers they planned to make for the nearest airfield and steal a two-seater. But first they urgently needed food.

During the second night they reached a shack overlooking a dam at Ommereith. Through the grimy window Swart saw a *feldgrau* figure eating honey and decided to raid the larder.

He leaped in, stick swinging; but the blow struck the soldier's shoulder and they crashed on to a truckle bed. From a dark corner there sprang another *soldat*, whose fist caught Fielding-Clarke as he reached the threshold. This man bolted the door, grabbed a Mauser rifle and yelled '*Handen hoch!*' Swart disentangled himself and surrendered—at which his wrestling partner promptly punched and kicked him to the floor.

The observer had been knocked into a nine-foot ditch and, weak from a recent bout of spotted fever, had difficulty in climbing out. He wanted to set light to the long grass bordering the hut but had lost his matches. The Germans poked their rifles through the window and fired as Fielding-Clarke miraculously collapsed below the muzzles.

So ended the bid for freedom, with flashlight photographs, questions from a general, and starvation rations in Fort Kameke at Metz, Karlsruhe, Landshut, and Holzminden (the last two being camps for 'bad boys'). By summer hundreds of RAF men would be following that trail, but none with more determination and grit.

This resolution was to be matched by that of Brigadier-General Newall. His physical valour had been acknowledged by award of the Albert Medal for controlling a blazing truckload of bombs. His efficiency as an administrator had caused his swift promotion. Now his moral courage as a leader became manifest. He ordered the start of Stage II, round-the-clock bombing.

# 3 *'... they offered burnt offerings thereon unto the Lord, even burnt offerings morning and evening.' (Ezra 3:3)*

The targets for February 18 were Thionville, 45 miles from base, the railway junction, north of Metz, and Trier. Both being along the well-guarded Moselle, nine DH 4s ran an AA gauntlet to make the day assaults. As the light failed eight Fees hit Thionville steel works and railway lines, setting some objectives alight with every type of bomb. Retaliation was vicious, and 2nd Lieut H. Jackson of Bradford and Air Mechanic J. G. Guyat of Watford paid the price of venturing too low.

Their spirit was not exceptional. At Trier the Mayor officially reported his admiration of a pilot who dived below the level of the surrounding hills, forcing the batteries to cease fire for fear of shelling the town. This was Lieut A. Wald (observer, Lieut S. M. Duncan), who finally scraped the roof-tops and planted two 112 lb bombs on tracks running through the railway station, which was then ignited by phosphorus canisters. The Chancery Court and market were also mangled.

Next morning, weather being promising, Mannheim was scheduled for 55 Sqn, but when mist crept up the Rhine Valley the leader diverted to Trier. One Four fell to fighters, which did not prevent barracks, workshops, and coal depots from suffering. And that night 16 (Naval) increased the damage in both Trier and Thionville.

Though partly accidental, this repetition threw fire brigades and repair squads into confusion and crowned Newall's strategy. The population believed there would be no cessation and pestered overwrought officials with demands for shelter or evacuation. Heedless of the anguish they caused, they scrawled their fears to relatives at the Front, so that a German pilot captured a few days later told RFC Intelligence that the moral effect had been very great. People, he added, who had put up with many privations were mentally in a worse condition to withstand air raids than were Londoners.

A wave of apprehension was rearing, and it would roll across the Fatherland no matter what dykes the outraged authorities could throw up. The swell spread wide from a target town, fear often being greatest in places where hearsay horrors could not be discounted by experience. Materially, only direct attack on specific objectives was satisfactory to Newall; but at this juncture any side benefits were valuable if they induced Whitehall to enlarge his command.

Pirmasens, a town producing Army boots and leather equipment, was defended by eight 9 cm guns whose ill-co-ordinated fire eight Fours avoided on February 20 to spread their 'sticks' across factories into private property where many civilians were injured. In five months it had been bombed three times with a total death roll of two. Yet an outcry arose, a typically overheated writer declaring: 'Every day we have to go three or four times to the cellar . . . for we are in a constant state of anxiety and excitement. The whole world could be destroyed before peace comes.'

Delegations transferred the burden of complaints to higher authority. They seemed, however, to be more mercenary than humanitarian. Social Democrats, for instance, asked in the Bavarian Lower House:

'Is the State Government aware that the population of Bavaria, and especially that of the Palatinate, has to suffer very material damage from aerial attacks which are constantly increasing? What does it contemplate doing to make good the damage to those concerned?'

Minister of Interior Brettreich, admitting the Palatinate had been considerably involved in recent air attacks, revealed his preoccupation with food shortages—'I wish to state for your assurance that little is to be feared from enemy incendiary bombs on our field crops.' He also introduced a bleat soon to become a chorus:

'Germans did not begin aerial attacks in this war. When our enemies cease attacks we shall also cease ours. With us it is mostly a matter of reprisals against which our enemies make unjustified aerial attacks on open towns.'

Apparently concern for wealth, expressed as monuments and

relics, was also the motive for a visit of Rhine mayors to General Headquarters where they begged for an end to raids on Allied cities because these only invited reprisals, which would be mounted tenfold when the *Amerikanische Schweinhunde* entered the field. Strikes and riots would be in proportion to the civilians killed. Above all, however, what about payment for loss of property?

Field Marshal Paul Von Hindenburg, the Commander-in-Chief, was furious, curtly dismissing the deputation. The effect of air raids on both sides had been greatly exaggerated, he barked. The Rhineland was not seriously threatened and at all costs the war would continue.

Loath though he was to detach any machines from strategic work Newall was perturbed by probing Gotha and Friedichshaven bombers to whom the thick woods around Ochey were at once a landmark and an obstruction. Near-misses had so alarmed 100's new CO, Major W. J. Tempest, that he removed the living quarters to the brush and rollered a fresh landing field.

Then blast hurled a Fee through the first production HP 0/100, No. 1455, on 16 (Naval) Sqn's tarmac. Hurriedly the old aerodrome, a mile away, was turned into a decoy studded with 'written off' aeroplanes for the benefit of Rumpler cameramen. Bomb-aimers, it was hoped, would be deceived by petrol blazes which would be lit electrically.

Bluff was too weak an answer to German intruders for men like Newall and Baldwin, and on February 26 they struck at an enemy lair; starting a series of blows which eventually would wither the Home Defence.

An EA surprised three Fees preparing at 6.20 pm for this mission to Frescaty aerodrome in the southern shadow of Metz. Hastily lights were doused and the Hun droned on to Nancy. While his cargo was spoiling the appetites of diners in Stanislaus Square the heavily burdened 'pushers' were dodging the green glare of 'flaming onions', a sinister but ineffective device of threaded explosives scattered by rocket tubes. As they sought the ground 12 searchlight beams unwisely followed them and outlined the old Zeppelin shed and hangars huddled among the trees. Everything then went dark as mist rolled in. Weeks went by before Newall learned that a 40 lb incendiary had burned out a hangar 100 yards long, 20 yards wide, and had frizzled all the aircraft.

Lacking information Tempest ordered another section to be

bombed-up, a difficult decision because the opacity had caused two Fees to overshoot Ochey.

HE bombs of the period were unwieldy and temperamental, even the little 20 lb Cooper fragmentation bomb being awkward to lift up to wing racks.

Until the second of release, fore and aft supports prevented the nose vane making its 25 revolutions which placed the firing pin against the detonator. For safety plenty of time and light was essential. But the 100 Sqn armourers had neither, and in the clammy gloom a vane was too lightly wedged . . . Blast and splinters shredded the Fee, pilot Capt C. Scudemore, MC, of Hammersmith, gunlayer F. Lem of Sheffield, Flt Sgt T. Green of Birmingham, Cpl A. McLeod of Glasgow, and Air Mechanic W. G. Cockburn of Co. Durham, by ranks and regions a cross-section of the squadrons at this time. Tempest closed down for the night.

Such incidents, no matter how tragic, could not be allowed to interfere with the larger plan. Newall, dining at Bainville, decided the Intelligence messages justified his moving to Stage III, the deep-penetration offensive. Nobody knew better what that might entail.

*   *   *

Behind the square Triplex glass windshield, the Aldis sight, and the Vickers gun-butt a DH 4 pilot insinuated his 150 lb cocoon. In front of his chin a dashboard held the air speed indicator, altimeter, thermometer, clock, hand pressure pump, inclinometer, map board, and a 5/17 magnetic compass illuminated in case night should race him home.

To the left there were arrayed petrol pipes and cocks, oil and petrol clocks, a pressure pump for the gravity tank, throttle, spark advance lever, and 'compensator'—a mixture regulator for high altitude.

To the right cables controlled the radiator shutter, a shelf held Very lights, and yet another pump activated the Constantinesco-Colley gear which synchronised the gun's fire with the passage of the propeller blades.

The observer, too, was not neglected. Around him revolved the steel Scarff ring with its ratchets for elevation and depression of one or two Lewis guns. His instruments were an ASI, altimeter, and throttle which, combined with joystick and rudder control grips, afforded him slender hope of crash-landing the machine should the pilot be knocked out. Aft of his sliding seat there was a camera well, besides shelves for plates and 97-round Lewis drums.

It would seem everything that could get a crew to its destination and back safely had been installed. Newall, however, was conscious that in the technological maze there was but one instrument to prevent aeroplane and man going 'missing' before they encountered the enemy. The aero compass was in its infancy. Thanks to the efforts of Dr Keith Lucas, FRS, at Farnborough it had been 'damped' to counter the Northerly Turning Error—the effect of gravity on the swinging weight of a compass card which caused big mistakes in reading. Still, it remained an elementary aid, and a frail one on which to depend for long-range operations.

The Admiralty had the Sperry gyro compass but was only now developing an aperiodic compass—which allowed very steady steering—plotting boards, and course-and-distance calculators, and there were no air sextants. Navigation was strictly Dead Reckoning.

In the Brigade there were some seasoned pilots who relied on their uncanny sense of direction. These quickly became very old when not very dead. A few degrees off track in northern France usually meant an overnight stay at a friendly farmhouse; at worst a tingling run to the nearest Allied trench. Outward-bound from the Nancy region a lost bomber would wander further and further into hostile territory; and inward-bound would bump a hillside.

Just the same the start of any mission, day or night, was something of a scramble into the wild blue yonder, the pilot's preparation amounting to no more than swinging his compass, plotting the course, and accepting estimated figures for wind direction and strength. Without wireless to recall him should a line squall arrive or the wind veer he was necessarily a fatalist.

Newall smothered his misgivings as March came in like a lamb. Now, if ever, was the hour to strike deep. The squadrons were sufficiently groomed and in good heart; squadrons that would soon have to set an example to reinforcements. They must be recognised as trail-blazers to faraway places.

Tantonville had not dried out, and engines and mechanics had to wrench the axles of 12 DH 4s out of the slush before they could take off for Mainz, in Hesse State at the junction of Main and Rhine, on March 9. Ten reached the town where Gutenburg had set up his printing press but which was now crammed with chemicals and leather, at midday and sent down a ton to explode on Hadenburg and the Reduit barracks. One 230-pounder sank a steam tug. Forty-one guns replied without dispersing the skilfully manœuvred formation. As one inhabitant put it, 'there was a regular panic'.

Next day as the Squadron took off for Stuttgart, the highly industrial capital of Württemberg on the Neckar River, the lead machine containing Capt J. B. Fox, MC, and Lieut S. S. Jones, MC, lit up. The rudder wires were burned through, and the Four smashed on the perimeter, Jones hauling his pilot clear seconds before the main tank ignited. The rest carried on, their 1¼-ton load being dumped between the Daimler motor works and a goods train. Several EA then appeared and in a brief exchange one spun out of control, to be followed by a Four.

Newall and, later, Trenchard were well served by the Secret Service and when the *Kreuz Zeitung* reported that no military damage had resulted 55 Sqn knew better. An agent said several erecting plants had been burned. Another, from Switzerland, counted the skeletons of 100 lorries. Five people had been injured.

Casualties were much heavier at Coblenz on the 12th, 70 civilians being killed or badly hurt, a party of them when a bomb fell in front of the post office. The nine Fours were aiming for the Friedrich barracks, where they did manage to kill four soldiers and wound twelve, and the Government automobile park. There was desultory opposition from Albatros D5s.

The flight was directed by Farrington, whose outstanding ability as a long-distance operator had been highlighted the previous year by a 3¾-hour reconnaissance at between 15,000 and 19,000 feet; and Newall, elated by his exertions, ensured that he would be appointed to the Distinguished Service Order for this new exploit.

The obverse was seen in a telegram sent to the Coblenz mayor by Louise, Dowager Duchess of Baden: 'With the greatest regret I learn of the severe visitation which has now for the first time affected Coblenz. I should like to express my heartfelt sympathies on this event. May God grant that this will be the last occasion on which you will be subjected to such a trial.'

Well-to-do families with more sense than faith became the

first evacuees received by the hospitable burghers of Bavaria and Saxony.

By all the laws of warfare 55's good luck could not continue, and on the 13th *Kampfeinsitzerstaffeln* broke the run. These guard squadrons, numbering 10 and termed *Kests*, had been formed exclusively for the Fatherland's protection and to back up the front line hunting units, the glamorous *Jagdstaffeln*. Since the beginning of the month they had been filtered along the Rhine and in Alsace-Lorraine, with single seaters—Albatros D5, Pfalz D3, Fokker DR 1 Triplane—and a few Halberstadt C3 two-seaters bringing each squadron's strength to twelve machines. The good equipment was not matched by the personnel, drawn from tired Western Front flyers and fledglings being tutored for sterner tasks.

*Kest* 4b under *Leut* Paul Leim was watching over Freiburg when the Tantonville boys sighted on to the munition works and barracks housing reserve troops but hit public buildings. The fighters climbed smartly but outpaced the Fours with difficulty. Tracers squiggled their mad designs around the bombers, which held firm in the defensive pattern evolved through desperate encounters with Manfred von Richthofen's Red Circus above No-Man's-Land.

In peaceful circumstances formation flying was an art as well as a drill, for engines seldom developed their factory-rated power, differences in rigging affected aerodynamics. Control response, at least on two-seaters, was invariably sluggish and the commander's signals needed to be obeyed instantly if a tragic tangle was not to ensue. Few were the pilots who did not have a memory of two intertwined machines showering the sky with their bones as they plummeted to their funeral pyre.

A moment's inattention and a neighbour's wheel might be through one's top plane or one's wing-tip sawing into another's tail section.

If station-keeping, involving constant adjustment of throttle and trim, was a heart-in-mouth business for any flight member the pressure on his leader was infinitely worse. Like the rest he had to watch for Archie bursts and EA, but additionally he would be measuring fuel consumption against distance, checking his compass, and making sure nobody was in trouble.

After run-up a flight could be airborne in 30 seconds, the leader climbing on full power to 700 feet and then throttling back to allow the others to pick up their 'dressing'. Still above the aerodrome his observer checked that everyone was in place and fired his first Very light, meaning 'leave rendezvous'.

Other colours might come later:

White (leader): east or west of the Lines, 'washout' (mission abandoned). Fired east of the Lines this also meant 'hold formation'.
Red (any other member): 'Attacked, need help'
Red (leader): 'Rally on me'
Green (anyone): 'Forced to return.' If from leader, deputy leader assumed command automatically.

Course set, every pilot would begin the neck-chafing rhythm of 'spotting the Hun in the sun', the sky being split into sections —port tip to centre section, straight ahead; centre section to starboard tip, ahead; starboard tip, above and curving round to port tip. Occasionally he would swing his tail to give the observer an opportunity to look for 'sneaky devils' climbing into a blind spot.

Battle joined, the pilots of the average well-rehearsed formation capable of keeping a span and a half apart tried not to open out to more than 100 ft. Observers would grit their teeth and hold their fire down to 200 yards. No. 55 had a standard hard to emulate.

The leader flew 40 yards to port of his wingmen, who were 15 ft higher, and 30 yards ahead of the slipstreaming deputy leader, whose starboard consorts were 15 ft lower. Further to the left were the rest of the flight, one or more of whom safeguarded the gap between sections. In this fashion streams of crossfire covered bellies and tail surfaces, and drilled pounds of metal into any fighter diving through the formation.

Three of the *Kests* broke into the orderly lines and each in turn went into the jerky spin that signified a wounded pilot or sliced controls. But the Germans persisted, well aware that their tanks were full and the enemy weary. Other fighters swarmed to their assistance, and two Fours tumbled—one being awarded to *Vfw* Weber of 4b as his fourth victory.

Vigorous counter-measures did not placate the *Frankfurter Zeitung* when it considered the latest incursion. 'It is obvious', thundered the leader writer, 'that the enemy by their attacks on open towns are trying to kill women and children . . . They are forcing us to return like for like; and then they shriek about barbarity and Hunnishness when German reprisals are more strong and effective than their challenge.'

Along the familiar route to Mannheim on March 18 the *Kests* gathered again, pouncing as the first wave concentrated on the Badische factory.

No tactic could be more upsetting. Bomb aimers might allow for the alterations in speed and height by which *flak* was avoided, but in air combat the aggressor enforced his rules and there was scant time for a pilot to place bombs accurately when he was watching the leader's signals, holding formation, co-operating with the gunner, and shooting at any EA coming head-on or diving across his nose.

He must fly blind while looking at the Negative Lens Sight, a piano-concave glass plate, 6 × 5½ in., mounted in the floor behind the rudder bar and giving a view of the country below. A pilot steered immediately up or down wind—preferably down wind because the extra push sped him over *flak* during his straight and level bombing run. And that was a cheering thought for any *Kest* hunter.

Somehow the Fours evaded the snipers long enough to score eight direct hits on the Badische factory, a huge column of black and white smoke rising from a cotton waste dump which burned for several hours. One bomb penetrated the Sulzer works and smashed hundreds of oxygen bottles. Observers also claimed two EA.

Seven heavy daylight raids by 63 machines in 10 days, with but four attackers brought down despite increasing resistance, startled the Germans in their hilly fastness as much as the first Zeppelin crossing to their seagirt fortress had shaken Londoners. Indeed there was more excuse for their shock.

The majority had spent the war many miles further from the rumble of guns than had the British, had been accustomed to land actions favouring their troops, to U-boats garnering a murderous harvest. Then just as the New World's intervention had dulled the brilliance of the military (though really diplomatic) triumph in Russia, when as their 'contribution to victory' they were ill-nourished and poorly clad, when lads were being drafted to fill the horrifying gaps torn on the Somme and Passchendaele, their homes began to crumble about them. By day millions untouched saw the even ranks of the enemy *en passage*, by night the red of his fires against the clouds.

Reaction differed from that of Londoners and Parisians, however, in that the Allies cried for tougher defences *and* offensives. No MPs or Deputies weakened their countries in the fashion of Herr Schultz, who cried in the Reichstag that the Government should take the initiative for an international agreement to prohibit aircraft raids outside the military zones. This view might be dismissed as that of a minority Radical but for the support he was given by the Council of Mainz and other authorities whose patriotism cannot be doubted.

Official attempts to reduce casualties were largely verbal, the police of Frankfurt anticipating trouble seven months away by urging householders to keep doors open so that innocent bystanders could dive for shelter. Counter-measures at factories were the 'priority' task. Dugouts were slowly being provided at plants, notably 45 elaborate but not deep ones at Thionville and 35 at Dillingen. Timbers and metal poles were reinforcing buildings and at Völklingen a dummy works covering 2000 metres was completed, and would twice be bombed in mistake for the Röchlingen complex to the north.

One cowardly reprisal which had been forecast by Trenchard and recently rumoured was exposed when *Flight* on March 21 reported: 'They [the Germans] consider themselves entitled to place British officers in whatever localities may be convenient, whether specially liable to air raids or not. It is stated that the British Government have naturally decided to adopt a similar course.'

The journal did not disclose its sources but in the House of Commons that afternoon they were not disputed. Instead Noel Pemberton-Billing, Independent MP for East Herts and self-styled Member for Air, asked whether Brettreich's comments on February 28 were accepted as an indication of our success; and would we redouble activity over German towns?

Andrew Bonar Law assured him that the Government was doing everything in its power to make raids effective.

Pemberton-Billing: 'Can this House understand that the raids which are being carried out are considered by HM Government as legitimate acts of war, and will not be discontinued in the event of the enemy squealing on the point of reprisals?'

Bonar Law: 'The House does understand that they are, in our

opinion, legitimate acts of war, and such acts are by no means undertaken as reprisals.'

That public statement of policy was true in military fact but scarcely in political spirit. The Government's original motives were to pay back Germany, show her that Zeppelins and Gothas were boomerangs, and persuade Londoners that their representatives were doing something of value to the war effort. These were psychologically unsound. It was Trenchard who had translated them freely in physical terms; Newall who had made them more purposeful. Without this soldierly disregard of what the front-line staff termed 'The Frocks' the atmosphere in the House would have been inward-looking, more mischievous, less militant.

Thus spurred, 55 Sqn swept across Mannheim at midday on March 24, toggling on to the Badische factory whose elimination, said a German supply officer, would have been a disaster. The best they could do was to plant a bomb three yards from a gas holder; but on the Ludwigshaven side of the river a petrol train exploded, 12 trucks being burned out. Flame-flecked smoke soared to 500 ft and could be seen 35 miles away. A stiff dog-fight took place, two Fours, including the deputy leader's, going down and another with a dead observer trailing ribbons of fabric into Tantonville. Two Huns were claimed as destroyed.

The bitterest of 55's encounters, and one which indicated worse in store, this raid had far greater repercussions on the ground. Summing up the distress and tension the 1½ tons of explosive created a resident wrote: 'The noise of the bombs and crashings was terrible. How will all this end? Others will be so affected that they will be ill all their lives, and still no peace.'

Twenty guns, 10·5 cm Ehrhardts and captured Russian 96·5s, were allotted to the Badische Fabrik, four more to the Frankenthal sugar factory. Between Ludwigshaven and the eastern slopes of the Vosges a further 26 were stationed. The 10·5 cm pieces were 12 ft long and capable of firing a shell costing £160 to 20,000 ft. Most of the crews, about 40 officers and men to a gun, were drawn from the *Landwehr* (home guard) but, as Germany's manpower situation became desperate, even these were replaced by men and boys unfit for any military duty.

They were housed, as elswhere, in spacious quarters 20 to 40 yards from the emplacements, which were revetted and had deep ammunition pits. Two command posts, linked with the area staff officer (*Stoflak*) at Mannheim HQ, operated underground.

Four other units deployed between four and eight machine guns in pairs on telescopic mounts or cement cones; seven balloon nets were sent up; and 12 searchlights—which the public imagined lit up their homes—began a nightly 'patrol'. A 20-to-30-minute warning for the Badische works was guaranteed. Never again would the Brigade have even a moderately quiet run.

Newall was conducting a simultaneous war of nerves. He had the initiative and the enemy, ill-served by French traitors or Alsatian agents, could never know his next ploy. That night some 100 Sqn pilots over Frescaty saw 16 aeroplanes waiting to attack and promptly plastered them with every size of bomb; but the Fees' main endeavour, with 13 airborne, was on the Metz-Sablons Triangle, eastern terminus of the German rail network to Antwerp.

By 9 pm they had distributed part of the cargo along the Metz Main No. 6 track, and then swept down on a train trying to pull away unobserved. The machines jumped in the up-blast as seven ammunition wagons erupted, the flames roaring on to the remaining trucks and bathing the sky with orange light. Two trucks lanced into adjacent houses, wrecking them and crumpling a gas holder. Exploding shells knocked a roof off a building and smashed machinery. Rows of houses bordering the railway were immediately evacuated, as were the Pioneer barracks where two of 100's parting bombs landed.

In daylight hundreds of soldiers cleared the débris, but traffic on 20 tracks serving Bensdorf, Courcelles, and Thionville was stopped for hours. Hardly a house within 50 yards of the train could be made fit for habitation.

Engine defects were bothering the Handley Pages, but Flight Commander F. K. ('Gus') Digby took off in his favourite, No. 3127, which had been operational for a year and now became the first aeroplane since October 1914 to comb Cologne, whose railway facilities, tool factories, cotton mills, and beet sugar plants greatly attracted VIII Brigade.

The flight lasted eight and a half hours and sent Wolff Agency propagandists into paroxysms about the danger to which the Gothic cathedral had been subjected—a church, incidentally, begun in 1248 and which the Prussians had not seen fit to complete until 1880. The city's *Oberbürgermeister,* Konrad Adenauer, much later to be German Chancellor, was not happy either.

An agent was more objective. Digby had put the electric power station out of action; and, 'the population was much affected, and information confirms previous reports that air raids are much dreaded and create panic and dissatisfaction which German authorities find increasingly difficult to cope with'.

Only two days elapsed before the exhausted, filthy, hungry toilers at Metz heard more aero engines, this time the full-throated song of the Rolls-Royce which preceded the specks that were 11 DH 4s. Again trucks leaped from their berths, tracks cork-screwed. But, far more serious in the shattered area, water mains were ruptured and supplies cut off.

Hammerings of this sort could be absorbed by a big town. In Metz they made any inhabitant feel that it could be only a question of days, maybe hours, before a bomb had his name on it. Sadly, Metz still contained many French people; but—as with the Resistants of World War II—they loathed the prime cause of their treatment more than those who were striving brutally to remove it.

Therefore, Newall was heartened but not surprised when he learned from a German POW lately in Metz that each raid brought to the Allied side more of those French who had been pro-German or apathetic about who ruled them.

Metz was 100's last assignment of the month. The squadron was to follow the northern thunder of heavy artillery as German divisions broke through between Lens and St Quentin, a massive stroke whose energy would not be spent for several weeks. Within three days 700 square miles were easily overrun, compared with 36 square miles after six months of squalid fighting in Haig's Flanders adventure.

Any and every aeroplane was needed to scatter reinforcements and munitions moving up in the dark along French rails. And it had been agreed that in grave circumstances the strategic machines could be so employed. In fact, the consequent move to Villesneux, an aerodrome west of Châlons-sur-Meuse, suited Major Tempest because a Rumpler had spotted wheel tracks on the new landing field at Ochey and a German strafe was an imminent prospect.

Meanwhile, 55 Sqn over Luxembourg, free of *flak* or fighters, ruled off their March droppings at 24,888 lb; and German authorities at last harkened to the mob.

Three stages of 'alert' were instituted. The first was *Luftgefahr* (danger of approaching aeroplanes) when unnecessary lights were covered, a 'brown out' rather than a blackout, and the anti-aircraft batteries warned.

As machines reached bombing range there would come the *Flieger Alarm.* All lights would be extinguished and civilians, including workers, would seek shelter. Signals varied, most places adopting the BEST rocket which, like the maroons in London, went off with a loud bang and a puff of white smoke. Sirens with a steady blast lasting two or three minutes reinforced them.

*Luftgefahr Veruber* (danger past) was notified by three successive blasts of three seconds. Only then might factories resume production, a delay which was to play Newall's game and whose effects were soon visible in supply figures.

Earth, concrete, and sandbags being thrown up for workers' safety would have been welcome sights to householders but when it was taking two months to build a gun emplacement there was little labour to spare on what as yet seemed an inessential. Paper was plentiful, and after April 2 many burghers found on their town hall walls a safety regulation both reasonable and cheap:

'It was observed on the occasion of the most recent air raids that quite a number of persons collected in the neighbourhood of the AA guns during the shooting, remaining there a considerable time. In view of the danger that such people run, under the circumstances it is hereby advised that, from the moment of the discharge of the first bomb, the presence of any civilian in the neighbourhood of the AA guns is strictly forbidden.

'It has, moreover, been repeatedly observed of late that the public, while bent on inspecting the AA installations, have trodden on and damaged the newly sown fields in the most inconsiderate manner. The county police and constables have therefore been instructed to inflict fines, in future, on all who transgress these regulations.'

Another proclamation, of the Royal Air Force's birth on April Fools' Day, eluded these readers. Nor was it received with *éclat* by VIII Brigade which noted that the regulation uniform would be khaki with pale blue and gold insignia of rank—and went on wearing its greasy and patched RFC and RNAS caps and jackets.

Weather was the big topic, spring weather which should have healed split lips and thawed bone marrows. More precisely, wind; which perversely whistled around hangars, pervaded canvas cockpits, and drifted five-ton bombers from their goal. Wind, which gave the harder-pressed German towns a respite for almost a fortnight, which diverted the Fours from the German HQ at Spa on April 5 and 11, and on the 12th, when, as an alternative, the disgusted pilots salvoed into Metz-Sablons.

Planners, too, experienced frustration because they now had available DH 4s with an extra tank under the pilot's wicker seat to give a flying time of $5\frac{1}{2}$ hours. One experimental machine, nicknamed The Pouter Pigeon, incorporated a huge belly tank which promised an even better range. But winds and mist persisted, so that the French railway stations and sidings at Juniville, Chaulnes, Nestle, Ham, Roye, Amagne-Lucquy, and Bethenville, to which 100 Sqn and 216 Sqn ('16' renumbered) paid attention on four nights, suffered no more ascertainable damage than a few minor fires.

Spreadeagled aeroplanes whose pilots had been unsighted by low-flying fog were a familiar find for shepherds and woodcutters, and some crews were entering more walking than flying time in their log-books. This was true even though men returning to Villesneux otherwise profited from clearer reference points such as the Marne river and Rheims Cathedral which German shells kept alight. Two died in accidents, another from pneumonia following exposure.

Amazingly, the lull did not calm German mayors. Bavaria, Hesse, and Baden were just as angry about the bombing of one town as they were when eight had received attention, some several times, during March. The 'cessation'-issue was again heard in the Reichstag; and Hindenburg authorised another harsh reply—the difficulties of German civilians were minuscule compared with those 'endured for three years with remarkable courage' by Allied citizens.

Except in this oblique phrase retaliation was not mentioned, nor was it worth mentioning. Since January a total of 11 Giants (Zeppelin Staaken multi-engined machines), had made three night attacks on Southern England; and from March 23 three Krupps 210 mm guns, mockingly known as Big Berthas after the manufacturer's wife, had lobbed 330 lb shells from St Gobain Forest into Paris. Haphazard and militarily worthless, these operations underlined the soldiers' preoccupation with their drive on the Western Front as much as their disregard of civilians' lives.

For *Flight* that was enough. '. . . it is no use deluding ourselves that the German High Command will listen to the protests of town councils or even of much more influential bodies or personages', snapped an editorial, 'until it has thoroughly demonstrated that the game of raiding open towns is not worth the candle.

'The constant bombardment of Paris by long-range guns is earnest enough of the fact that the psychological effect of "frightfulness" on civilian populations is regarded by them as a weighty factor in war . . . We shall have to perpetrate quite a lot more frightfulness yet to bring them to a better frame of mind.'

Elsewhere in London action was about to accompany the words.

# PHASE II

## *'Independent of God?'*

# 4 '. . . *The First was like a lion and had eagle's wings . . .*' *(Daniel 7:4)*

Civilians passing the Hotel Cecil on April 25 and startled by RAF staff officers shouting down to them that Whitehall had won a victory, that Rothermere was finished, did not realise that they were in at the birth of the Air Force as an operational entity. Still less did they imagine the squalid interplay which had preceded the happy event.

That was heralded when Trenchard found the Air Minister refused to define the precise nature and scope of the Chief of Staff's duties. It began with an arbitrary instruction to ransack the other Services for RAF manpower, irrespective of war needs, and continued when the Hotel Cecil's 1000 rooms quickly filled with healthy young protégés of Influential People.

It progressed with Trenchard making a clean sweep of the wingless wonders, and Rothermere retaliating by turfing out fire-tested commanders, among them future Air Marshals Dowding, Ludlow-Hewitt, and Longcroft. Piffling complaints culled, and sometimes solicited, from cranks fluttered into Trenchard's trays, the Minister having caused them to be passed down or, worse, up. Simultaneously the anti-Haig campaign gathered pace.

These harassing moves in the Power Game, familiar to Fleet Street editorial executives who have outlived their usefulness, alternated with periods of 'The Freeze' when Rothermere —admittedly sickened by the loss of two gallant soldier sons— was 'not available' to his chief adviser.

The break came when, without consulting Trenchard, Rothermere blithely offered the Navy 4000 aircraft for anti-submarine patrols—although not a tenth of that number was spare or even serviceable. After a week Sir Eric Geddes, First Lord of the

Admiralty, asked Trenchard why he was not delivering them. The following day, March 19, Rothermere received Trenchard's resignation, but asked for deferment of its execution for a few days until fresh arrangements—which he hinted might involve his own departure—could be made.

Forty-eight hours later the Germans launched their push and on April 10 Rothermere abruptly foreclosed, suggesting that Trenchard resume command in France.

To Trenchard, who had recently written to John Salmond 'you are splendid', the offer was odious. He could only kick himself for tumbling into a corner from which he now appeared to be quitting a key post at the height of the battle.

Out-manœuvred, he whiled away the next crucial week mooning in his flat and on park benches. His only activity was a Statement of Case addressed to the Prime Minister. Combined with the effect of a wildly inaccurate Rothermere circular about RAF policy this convinced Lloyd George that Rothermere should be helped to decide his own future.

At last Trenchard had a friend in court. The new Air Minister was Sir William Weir (later Viscount Weir), the Glasgow engineer-magnate in charge of aircraft production and nothing if not a patriot. Long before the Smuts Report he had argued that 'bombing aeroplanes will drop more HE behind the German lines, for the same cost and at a longer range than howitzers, since a bomb needs less steel than a shell, and petrol is cheaper than cordite'. As the struggle wore on he became convinced that the war would be won above the Fatherland. He was also sure the victor would be Trenchard, and not by a jot could the nominee's own doubts modify that optimism.

He had inherited Frederick Sykes as CAS and, politically canny, resolved not to upset the appointment. Instead he gave Trenchard the choice of RAF Inspector Generalships, either Overseas or Home, and of GOC Middle East.

There was a fourth prospect—the independent command of long-range bombing forces in France, 'the strength and final development of which will represent a big command, particularly if associated with America'.

Trenchard displayed his worst traits, obstinacy and pettishness, in his varied objections to these roles, which he suspected had been manufactured. He was logical, however, when he asserted that Newall—'one of the best generals in the air service'

—was doing as well as anyone could at Ochey. London-based administration would only mean divided command; and the French, already antipathetic to strategic bombing, would refuse to deal with yet another British leader.

Despite Weir's assurance that he was truly needed and that none of the jobs had been contrived to 'quell the agitation' Trenchard remained undecided. The story goes that he succumbed when, visiting the Green Park in 'civvies' on May 8, he overheard two senior naval officers describing his resignation as desertion. Within hours Weir had his acceptance of the independent command, and guaranteed his direct support—an important, although irregular, factor because Trenchard did not like the clever Sykes, who he considered feeble and devious.

A week later the General, accompanied by journalist Maurice Baring, a veteran member of his staff and his confidant, found his autumn seeds blossoming. The wastelands had become five vast aerodromes sufficient for 30 bomber squadrons, basically provisioned and in many cases bordered by living quarters, depots, and service tracks. He re-established good relations with the Americans who appreciated that, unlike Allied Army commanders, he had no desire to superimpose his flag on theirs.

The other Ally was a different proposition. Weir might declare, 'the French must give ground . . . If you have any trouble I will get the PM to convince Clemenceau' (the French Premier). Indeed he did ask War Cabinet approval for the formation of an inter-Allied bombing force, to which Georges 'Tiger' Clemenceau gave his tentative blessing. But in the field Trenchard discovered that the French Army air component, dominated by Foch, was less amenable. 'For instance, if I ask the French railway authorities for facilities to bring trains into the neighbourhood with my stores, the answer I may get is "What are you? We know nothing about you",' he complained to Weir. 'This will take place over all matters, roads, supplies, maps, and other items . . .'

On the representations of Duval, now Deputy Chief of French General Staff with administrative responsibility for the air service, Foch refused to admit the existence on his home soil of 'an irregular air force' under orders from Whitehall—a philosophy echoed by Charles de Gaulle when in World War II he resented the British Special Operations Executive organising Resistance cells in his Occupied country.

Trenchard sighed for du Peuty, but he, unable to stomach the Army's neglect and misuse of its aviation, had returned to his Zouave regiment to die on the barbed wire of Chemin-des-Dames. Another champion had to be enlisted, and quickly.

Meanwhile, there was dismay at Tantonville to which 99 Sqn (CO, Major Lawrence A. Pattinson, MC) had flown their Siddeley Puma-powered DH 9s despite valve springs broken during the 240-mile flight from St Omer near the NW coast of France—an alarming foretaste of the ordeal ahead. Carburettors were also defective, so that above 10,000 ft the average and prohibitive petrol consumption reached 15 gallons an hour.

Otherwise the aeroplanes were strong, comfortable, and handy. A few inches of fabric separated pilot and observer, the main fuel tank—covered in doped fabric to drain off petrol in case of a hit—being behind the engine. Instead of being built into the nose the radiator was fitted ventrally before the undercarriage and could be raised or lowered by the pilot. Two 230 lb bombs, or an equivalent weight, could be housed internally; but in practice the Nines with half that load took 75 minutes to scale the requisite operational height of 14,000 ft.

Not many of the aviators had seen active service and Pattinson put them to copying 55 Sqn's formation tactics, so that their first bombing sortie was not possible until May 21. There was no indication that eventually '99' would lose 42 officers in action alone.

Metz had its wounds viciously opened on May 17 with the arrival of 12 Fours above the main station, on to which tumbled a ton of explosives. Five bombs tore up tracks and razed a goods shed. The worst of the havoc centred on an express train with steam up.

Alongside one carriage a guard of honour of cavalry and infantry was arrayed when a thin-cased 230-pounder buried its yellow nose in the platform. Between the tail fins there was a fuse timed for two and a half seconds, and nobody outpaced it.

When the acrid smoke cleared 11 officers lay tangled in the smouldering train. Bloody fragments of another 30 soldiers and three civilians were strewn around the station. Fifty-four innocent bystanders were wounded, and minutes later their misery would have been shared by the men they had gathered to see. But again the Kaiser's time-table had saved him from the Independent Force.

That night 216 Sqn, and, having returned to Ochey, 100 Sqn, raided another station at Thionville. After weaving through the ceaseless beams of 17 searchlights they knocked out tracks and the telephone control. Much of their load dropped into the town square, killing 35 people, two-thirds of them soldiers. A Fee crashed, and with a gesture of chivalry rare in this sector a German aeroplane dropped a message across the Lines to say that 2nd Lieut J. C. Williamson of Oswestry and Lieut N. F. Penruddocke of Eastbourne were unhurt.

The efficiency of 55 Sqn was exemplified next morning when Capt F. 'Billy' Williams and Lieuts J. R. Bell, A. S. Keep, Walmsley, Reynolds, and Wild set up a squadron distance record with the first daylight attack on Cologne for nearly four years. Using cloud cover to the full the six Fours avoided interceptors until by 9.20 am they had battered 38 buildings, among them the infantry barracks, gymnasium, water and electricity works, and the Rathaus. Forty burghers were killed, 100 injured, numbers being caught in the city's two markets. Trolley cars ran away because women drivers neglected to switch off current, and 17 passengers died when a 'tram' received a direct hit in Rotgerbach.

Wheeling from the destruction Williams' flight was engaged by strong formations but sent two Huns into a spin and outdistanced the rest. Elated, Trenchard wired 'Alec' Gray: 'Splendid. Am coming to see you shortly! Give my congratulations to all pilots and observers.'

For the Cologne *flak* commandant there was no bouquet. His guns were not brought into action until the Fours were distant, and when they did retaliate they shot down a German fighter. In the Reichstag Deputy Kuckhoff berated the defenders, and *General Major* von Weisburg replied:

'The inhabitants were not given the alarm in time to enable them to take shelter as they would have done. The enemy attack seemed at first to be intended for Trier and then for Coblenz. Meanwhile, although no news had been received, the inhabitants should have been given the alarm. This was not done.

'With regard to initial limitations of air raids the following can be stated:

'The Germans cannot make the first approaches to the enemy to stop raids on towns outside the war zone. The German Government on the contrary must wait for the enemy to approach it. Should such an offer be made it would be conscientiously examined by Germany, and at the same time it would be considered what qualifications would have to be made to secure that German interests should not be affected.'

That was satisfactory to the *Kölnische Volkszeitung*, whose realistic leader writer said that Cologne was a fortress and citizens would have to adapt their nerves to unpleasant surprises from the air. 'The naive notion that our enemies would stop their bombing raids the minute the Germans stopped theirs would certainly meet with sharp disappointment should we make the attempt,' he added. 'By so doing the German Army Command would only one-sidedly lose a means of reprisal which was widely called for by the German nation themselves.'

The sluggish *flak* CO was dismissed his post, and the defences stiffened with 28 guns and 21 searchlights, which also covered the works at Leverkusen, Oplandau, and Mülheim. But the stable door was still off its hinges, and before the month ended Cologne's industrial capacity declined by 50 per cent.

Prompt warnings also brought their problems. Seven Handley Pages shook up Mannheim's Oppau factory during the early hours of May 22; and no sooner had the sirens screeched than professional thieves and casual looters broke into stores and upstairs rooms vacated by shelterers. Barely 24 hours elapsed before the gangs resumed their personal war by the glare of hydrogen supplies ignited at Oppau. Villains, however, did less harm than 11 bombs which made the factory suspend work for two days.

At Conz railway repair shops were demolished. At Thionville FEs started fires, and at Dillingen and Saarbrücken between 1.35 and 4.20 am bursts were observed all over the towns. Two bombs caused 23 casualties in the Saarlouis barracks. Visibility deteriorated rapidly as the 'pushers' neared home and, squeezing into the unfamiliar aerodrome of Epiez, four crashed.

Now, shrugging off their mechanical snags, 99 Sqn were ready for blooding. They had raided Metz twice from 14,000 ft, registering a number of hits, but they first sparred with the enemy over the Thyssen blast furnaces at Hagondange on May 24. Only two B Flight machines managed to join the six of Capt W. D. Thom's A Flight. Their presence became important when eight Albatros D5s swept in at 200 yards' range behind, only to have their ardour cooled by the compact and regular bunching of the DH 9s. One Hun, stitched by crossfire, dived over the vertical for 4000 ft until swallowed by cloud. Thereafter the Albatros melted away and, although in ever-increasing pain from leg wounds, 2nd Lieut M. A. Skinner and a fellow pilot, 2nd Lieut O. Jones, stayed in formation. AA took up its task and, combined with strong winds, spoiled the bombing. Damage to several machines reduced the effective strength of 99 Sqn from 15 to six.

Three days later 14 were available to tackle Bensdorf station, 16 miles over the Lines. The target was narrow, lay east and west, and there was a tough north-east wind blowing; but three bombs excavated a section of the track and others set light to a building. Four Nines were forced back by engine trouble, another shot down by *Vfw* Krüger.

The remaining daylight hours of May were bedevilled by fast-moving but thick cloud, turbulence, and haze. The additional peculiar hazards of defective vacuum controls and broken exhaust valve springs—averaging three out of four engines on sorties—depressed 99 Sqn, and the mechanics became worn out from lack of sleep and hard labour. Nor were the Nines with the brand new 104 Sqn under Major J. C. Quinnell, which had reached Azelot on the 20th, in better shape.

It was the dark that Metz, Thionville, and adjacent townships had to fear. The guns raked the Handley Pages and ubiquitous Fees, although perverse weather proved a surer deterrent, but invariably after the damage had been done. As at Kreuzwald, where between 10 and 11 pm on May 27 the crews of 12 FEs heard the mighty explosions in the electricity station pierced by twenty-seven 112-pounders and gazed into molten splodges caused by 10 incendiaries. The uproar would have been greater had not five of their companions not aborted through loss of power and sight.

Ninety guns, among them seven motorised sections, roared or stuttered their anger along the Saarburg-St Avold-Metz barrier. Yet only one shell was effective. It burst under the engine of a Fee flown by Lieut L. D. Kirk of Dalmuir, who felt the revolutions magically disappearing. Seconds later he was skidding on to the dark turf, unable to benefit from his Holt flare for fear of summoning German troops. The touchdown was rough and not until the observer, 2nd Lieut W. Richards of Llandudno, had recovered from a knock on the head could they plan to escape.

Miles from help, in wild country sown with traps, shocked, half-frozen, foodless, and with only soft flying soles to their boots these young men doggedly tramped south-westwards, periodically turning aside to avoid gun emplacements and similar obstacles. Towards dawn they stumbled into rolls of barbed wire and sacrificed their one-piece Sidcot suits so they might crawl across the leather. Soon afterwards they halted abruptly on the lip of a German trench and realised they had reached a forward area.

Bypassing it they sought shelter under a hedge in No-Man's-Land and there, suffering from thirst, they stayed for a tense 16 hours. On the resumed march they resolved to follow the River Moselle but were badly scratched by more entanglements. Thankfully they quit the open country for a wood.

Simultaneously bullets whined overhead. Flinging themselves to the ground they wriggled through tall grass to the river bank, slugs still cutting the foliage about them. Richards insisted on plunging across to locate and clear obstacles before his pilot, a poor swimmer, entered the chilly water. Once over they heeded the seductive wink of Lighthouse C by which they made an unorthodox return to 100 Sqn via French HQ at Lixiéres.

They were needed; for a few hours later 2nd Lieut V. R. Brown of Jamestown (USA) and Air Mechanic A. Johnson of Dublin, who had helped to stoke a fire at Metz South station, were taken prisoner before they could disentangle from the wreckage of their Fee.

While the moon minions were justly asleep Trenchard explained to his future commanders the structure of the Independent Force and what he required of it.

Cloud flying, he insisted, must be practised assiduously, because soon he would expect squadrons to bomb through the overcast. As for night flyers, no longer would their maximum efforts be confined to moonlight periods. Dark nights, long journeys; bad visibility, day attacks—that was the harsh policy.

Those with Western Front experience were reminded that Trenchard inspired, cajoled, and if necessary bludgeoned his COs and crews into working his will. So long as the equipment could carry them they would go, and for the most part with determination and good heart.

The General's other injunction, that friendly relations be cultivated with the French, was evidently more difficult of accomplishment. Attending a sub-committee of the Supreme War Council at Versailles, Trenchard made little headway towards acceptance of his 'irregular' command.

Indeed Haig's reaction was to advise his former subordinate

that only by deeds could he convince the French that the Independent Force was useful to them and not an encumbrance. Thus far did his Francophobia overcome his loathing of the IF.

Appreciating that the Army was absorbed with the Germans' recapture of Chemins-des-Dames, the turning of the Aisne line, and the consequent fact that the enemy was securely concentrated barely 10 miles north of Château Thierry, at the conference table the new British Chief of Air Staff sought to allay the fears of General Duval.

Sykes, coldly precise in manner but indecisive of action, insisted that in any emergency the IF would be placed unreservedly at Foch's disposal. He had only to ask. But Duval retorted that 'from a military standpoint orders were usually better than requests'.

The British force was independent. 'Independent of whom?' he jeered. 'Of God?'

Resenting the *fait accompli* represented by the VIII Brigade he withheld support for the wider scheme, whose primary object he interpreted as the neglect of the Boche field forces unleashed at the heart of France. Every aeronautical resource should be employed; and he doubted the wisdom of Britain's concentrating on bomber output—even if that satisfied the BEF and Royal Navy.

The talks broke down, Weir discovered Lloyd George's resolution weakening, and, prepared for a tussle, he privately observed to Trenchard that the Government would topple should it cease to belabour Germany.

Thereafter Trenchard wooed French area commanders and completely won the courtly General Noël de Castelnau, more than Pétain the saviour of Verdun and presently leader of the French Eastern Armies from whose ground the IF took wing.

Local accord had no effect on the peculiar happening of May 29. Without knowledge of the crews, who would have been quite relieved had they heard, Cologne was erased from the target list for 55 Sqn. Thionville replaced it. But the change did not elude righteously amazed questioners in the House of Commons on June 3. For Cologne's Roman Catholic Mayor had initiated a subterranean move which had crumbled the resistance of Protestant Lloyd George.

Under the probes of Mr R. McNeill and Capt Carr-Gomm the plot emerged: the Vatican had appealed for Cologne's immunity from British bombing on May 30, the Feast of Corpus Christi; and had received the assurance.

Captain Carr-Gomm twisted his Honourable and Gallant knife: Had the attention of the Vatican been drawn to the shelling of Paris on Good Friday and to the London air raid on Whit Sunday?

To which Andrew Bonar Law could only respond: 'The appeal was received by the French and British Governments and the reply in the terms already announced was sent after consultation and in agreement with the French Government. The staff of the Air Ministry was also consulted.' (With what result he did not say!)

'The action of the Germans in shelling Paris in spite of our undertaking will not be forgotten, in the event of any similar appeal being made in the future.'

He added that there was 'a great deal to be said on both sides in regard to an appeal of this kind'. The Government had not asked the Germans for reciprocity—'We were doing this because we thought it was right so to do.'

Colonel Thorne: 'Do you not think the Germans think we are a lot of fools?'

Clearly the Germans did, for in their country Corpus Christi was not celebrated on May 30 . . .

Glumly Trenchard could only conclude that this was not the way for the British to run a war.

# 5 *'He hath laid a siege against me . . .' (Micah 5:1)*

Despite political flabbiness, disunity among GHQs, and the DH 9 fiasco there was euphoric unanimity in both technical and lay Press about the importance of the task assigned to the Independent Force.

*Flight* knew it was 'about to witness one of the transformations which come only once in centuries when a new order of weapon conclusively proves its power'. But it was the *Daily Mail* which found the phrase: 'Siege by Air'.

Both notions were grandiose and premature, primed perhaps by the summer weather, which might also have heartened 99 Sqn had the heat not sapped the scant energy from their struggling engines. Jaded flight commanders, invariably confronted by three-quarters of their formation forced-landing with fractured valve springs, reviled the sun which added cracked cylinder heads to their worries. To relieve the strain they agreed to cross the Lines below a customary bombing level, but were then shaken by prevalent 30 mph winds at the elected 13,000 ft. Fitters now worked 14 hours a day; and an expert sent out by the Siddeley Company offered no remedies—which were then devised by squadron members.

A brief respite was granted on June 5 when the squadron joined the other day units at Azelot, an excellent aerodrome but one with approach roads crammed by slow-moving French-Algerian, Cochin Chinese, Indian, Italian, and Russian labour gangs whose toil never seemed to be done.

The following day the Independent Force officially came into being. But, the winds unwilling, its history began inconspicuously with forays to Coblenz and Thionville by the de Havillands.

Practice was making '99' as near perfect over the target as the

Negative Lens Sight would allow. When four out of 12 machines reached Thionville on the 7th their leader, Capt P. C. Purser, MC—a Somme veteran, suffering from an old lung wound—was delighted to observe detonations on a road bridge and rail tracks. Station-keeping, too, had improved. Only the engines were obstructive.

Watching them from Brigade HQ 10 minutes before they crossed the Lines the following day Newall declared he had never seen a more efficient assembly of 12 aircraft. But even as he lowered his binoculars three Nines broke down. In the fourth Garrity became the first casualty of another peculiar defect—carbon monoxide poisoning from the exhaust pipe insidiously voiding fumes in line with his face. Semi-conscious he landed his observer safely before being lifted into a hospital-bound tender. His name joined that of 20 mechanics, on the sick list for a variety of Puma-induced complaints from septic cuts to plain exhaustion.

Whatever their respective sores the IF squadrons had not only to maintain the pressure but to increase it. Trenchard had spoken.

Installed in his 17th-century L-shaped château with twin magician's cap towers on the hill above Autigny-la-Tour, four miles north-east of Neufchâteau, the General had two propositions before him. He could mount continuous attacks on every big German production centre in succession until each was razed or its work force driven out. Or he could blast at any promising target within his reach. Either way his objective was 'the breakdown of the German Army in Germany, its Government, and the crippling of its source of supply'.

He chose the second plan, because:

'1. It was not possible with the Forces at my disposal to do sufficient material damage so as to completely destroy the industrial centres in question.

'2. It must be remembered that, even had the Force been still larger, it would not have been practical to carry out this unless the war had lasted another four or five years, owing to the limitations imposed on long-range bombing by the weather.'

Not until the final quarter of World War II would that reasoning be outmoded, and prior to that revolution several brilliant commanders with between 22 and 26 years' experience of aerial warfare would fail to see what he foresaw with only three. Consider the bare facts on which Trenchard made his judgment.

Before Newall's enterprise several air arms had conducted spasmodic raids on less remote targets, in weather varying from excellent to poor. The German Gothas—bravely overcoming the psychological bar of the sea—had persevered with raids on London, upsetting the public far more than industrial output. Newall, operating over difficult country in fair to suicidal conditions, had been a catalyst of fear but hardly of economic or political collapse.

Therefore the success of Trenchard's own offensive would be at best a fringe benefit. He could rip the sociological fabric of Germany, stirring dissension, cracking industrial walls, and draining Western Front arteries. Patriotic fervour might be subdued by logic, if by infiltrating bombers to any town at will he could convince the enemy that a German war meant war inside Germany.

Immediately, he needed more day squadrons. Four-fifths of the night raiders' value would be wasted supposing industry and commerce became geared to intensive daylight working and arranged sleeping quarters out of town. German heads had to be kept down all the time, but not in bed. Besides, although casualties were fewer among night bombers they had more difficulty in finding their targets and in observing results. Without the de Havillands *Kests* would be relieved of patrols and appear on Salmond's borders.

Already Intelligence from Hunland was startlingly accurate, especially in centres such as Metz, occupied since the Franco-Prussian War. Messages were delayed, however, and extra daylight photo-reconnaissance was a necessity.

Trenchard, perhaps the least articulate man in a sphere where except as clubs words have always been suspect, was before his time in desiring his most junior flyer to understand the nature and quality of the task assigned him.

There can be no negative views about this towering figure who was strictly 'Regular Army' before he learned to fly, badly, at the then advanced age of 40. His thunderous voice had earned him the nickname of 'Boom' by those—and that meant almost everyone—unaware that a Boer bullet had cost him a lung. His staccato verbal shorthand paralysed subalterns, quelled field officers, and bewildered all but a few ultra-perceptive Staff aides. Even today one faction of those who served him in RFC, RNAS, and IF squadrons calls him 'butcher', profligate of men as he was sparing of imagination. The other considers him a benign phenomenon who, belonging to an age when it was still noble to stake all on one's convictions, kept a powerful and ruthless enemy at bay by inspiring a band of oil-stained Cinderellas with the vision of their high destiny. The second notion contains a fair amount of truth.

Undoubtedly Trenchard possessed the magnetism of a great military leader, and, while utterly devoid of the Staff temperament, he was a gifted planner.

For the IF he introduced the most detailed system of briefing so far attempted by British aviation. Intelligence officers provided and kept up-to-date all conceivable information about factories turning out aeroplanes, engines, poison gas, and ancillary products. Text was accompanied by maps, plans, photographs, and, when necessary, models. Routes to take account of every type of weather and wind pressure were available for each target, with surrounding defences pinpointed.

Apparently he did not make use of film; but otherwise his target plots were equivalent to those for the 1000-bomber raids on Hitler's Reich.

Without wireless communication between machines—radio telephony of Salmond's 22 and 88 Squadrons was experimental—and with the opaque skies expected in autumn, inevitably formations would become separated and even lost. They need not waste bombs, however, if given specific No. 2 targets. So as primary alternatives Trenchard chose railways—because, as he reported later, 'the Germans were extremely short of rolling stock and also some of the main railways feeding the German Army in the West passed close to our Front . . .' They were also easy to locate at night, blast furnaces becoming second alternatives for the same reason.

Natural hazards were therefore circumvented to some extent. Their immediate influence was negligible compared with the growing menace of the *Kests*, whose motley collection had been supplemented by a rocketing interceptor out of the Siemens Schuckert *Werke*. Recently Ernst Udet, at that time Germany's third-ranking ace, had tested the SS D3 from Metz and it was marked as equipment for *Kests* 2, 4A, 4B, 5, 6, and 8. The 160 hp Siemens Halske rotary engine—oiled by *ersatz* fuel—had been overheating and after modifications the rotund V-strutter was still not speedy in level flight, but its fast-climbing capacity and manœuvrability could give de Havilland pilots nasty surprises.

Just the same Trenchard dismissed the SS D3 as a tactical problem. He who had always carried the war to the enemy was haunted by the silver twinkle of reconnaissance Rumplers training superlative Zeiss lenses on his aerodromes from 20,000 ft and by the heavy bomber COs who awaited the revealing plates. They could ruin the IF before it became airborne. Unless he struck first.

He dropped the final, and key, piece of his plan into place—unrelenting assault on German bomber and fighter airfields. Appreciating, as few commanders have ever done, the resilience of the German war machine he estimated that by 'the spring and early summer of 1919' half of the Force would be diverted to this dangerous and negative work.

In the squadrons missions became routine, the yellow 'eggs' tumbling regularly on to Metz, Thionville, Coblenz, Conz, Hagondange, Dillingen, and Trier. The hazards of AA, fighters, collision, conking engines, and altitude sickness were too insistent for monotony. But the sun lent a clownish aspect to the blotchy, oil-logged, fabric of the machines. It softened the devastation wrought at Dillingen by 99 Sqn on June 13 when Lieut Marthinius Papenfus won the DFC by taking command of 14 machines after Capt A. D. Taylor's Nine dropped back with a snapped magneto drive.

Ten aeroplanes of A and C Flights made the target, a stream of bursts being recorded across railway lines, buildings, blast furnaces, and the Dillinger Huttonn Factory. 'Large flames' were later identified by Intelligence as the gusher from a burst water main.

Simultaneously 55 Sqn was salvoing into the Trier iron factory and other installations. A swarm of EA gathered but exchanged two of their number for a DH 4 in flames.

Four civilians were killed and eight wounded, a casualty roll whose lightness did not stem the fury of Trier city councillors. In vain the *bürgermeister* denied that AA efficiency had lessened, that shells were being restricted, and that firing ceased when *Kests* were within range. He deemed it necessary to sound the air-raid alarm every day 'otherwise inhabitants will think the warning system has broken down'. Evidently the poor man was in a state of shock.

Trying for Metz on June 16 99 Sqn encountered thick clouds like half-furled sails at 15,000 ft and these were the forerunners of banks which built up and filled in all areas for more than a week, the towering bastions dissolving only to let down torrents of blinding rain.

The 'dud' time was happily exploited, however, with carefree crews bundled into Crossley tenders splashing to and from the restaurants and estaminets of Nancy, and days of sleep for the bulk of air mechanics. The Siddeley specialists having let them down one energetic team fitted large carburettor air intake pipes to DH 9 6202, and on test with full war load the machine reached 3000 ft in 5¼ minutes instead of in seven minutes with the factory fitting. In the Azelot Mess 'Blighty', at times the nickname for all that was worthwhile, had a bitter taste on the tongue.

That applied even to those who might briefly sample its drab serenity. The middle-class home was a bleak place with fathers vicariously winning the war, kippers and bacon replaced by haricot bean fritters and five-course dinner by sauce-flavoured soup, thin slices of the weekly ¾ lb meat ration, and barley rissoles. Pubs dispensed denatured beer at 9d a pint from noon to 2.30 pm and opened for between two and three hours in the evening.

Houses bore signs of disrepair, streets the litter from endless food queues. Shop-window dressers confined themselves to war-paint. William Whiteley Ltd, Universal Providers, coaxed the 'well-dressed woman' to don 'smart overalls in good quality casement cloth for 7s 11d' and 45s National Service Boots 'ideal for ladies engaged in war work of every description'. Deprived of both pins and elephants Harrods had shelved its world-renowned slogan, its most attractive offer being the weekly carriage of the regulation 2 oz of tea for 10s to anywhere in Britain.

From many hangers the Standard Suit drooped, despite having been cut from 'the same material and pattern as a length recently purchased by the King'. But at £2 17s 6d it aroused longing, both spiritual and financial, in RAF officers who could be fitted 'within 48 hours' with the new Service jacket (105s) and knicker breeches (55s).

The halfpenny *Daily Mail* and the penny *Times* had doubled in price and were waging war on caterpillars—'the Huns in your garden'—which were ravaging the nation's fruit throughout the Home Counties. As the male call-up had reached the 51-year-old and women were too busy as milk roundsmen, transport crews, and factory hands to wave smouldering paper above the invaders' noses, the official remedy, orchards remained infested.

Undoubtedly the best daylight entertainment was at the Central Criminal Court where Noel Pemberton-Billing, the mercurial 'MP for Air', was defending his indefensible but amazingly upheld charge of perversion against actress Maud Allen. Co-author of this allegation was an RAF officer, American-born Captain Harold Sherwood Spencer, his contribution to the prolonged case being the recollection that Prince Wilhelm of Wied owned a list of 40,000 presumed British perverts—including, he mentioned apologetically, presiding judge Lord Darling—for the blackmailing purposes of German Intelligence. Regrettably few leave-takers acquired seats, the Old Bailey just then being as popular as the National Gallery, where turnstiles broke down under crowds escaping the bleak streets.

With night came the grey-out in memory of Zepps and Gothas, although the theatres were never brighter inside. Early in the month *A Little Bit of Fluff* ended at the Criterion but the record-breaking *Chu Chin Chow* was at His Majesty's, *The Maid of the Mountains* at Daly's, and at the Prince of Wales' 'the best laugh in London', *Fair and Warmer*. Gerald du Maurier was in *Dear Brutus* at Wyndhams, Arthur Bourchier as Old Bill in officer-cartoonist Bruce Bairnsfather's play, *The Better 'Ole* at the Oxford.

The IF contingent might have found some affinity with *Seven Days' Leave* (Lyceum), *Going Up* with Joseph Coyne at the Gaiety, and *By Pigeon Post* starring Arthur Wontner and Madge Titheridge at the Garrick. But undoubtedly they would have chosen Wee Georgie Wood & Co in *Some Detective* at the Victoria Palace in preference to *The Kaiser—Beast of Berlin* for which the civilians eagerly paid from 1s to 7s 6d at the Scala.

If the 'ginger beer' gin of mushrooming night clubs did not prematurely terminate a leave, Press correspondents' vignettes from France could turn the trick. Even the *Daily Mail,* most aviation-conscious of dailies, offered this recruiting-poster impression of the Independent Force . . .

'The pale beams of searchlights pay their homage to these great eagles of the moon. Scintillating chains of emerald balls rise to greet them in their passage. Shells mingle their red twinkling with the clear stars which burn in the velvet o' the night. The night bombers are happy.'

From such sentiments many fled to the duty ferry and reality, whose terrors were softened by the purposeful comradeship bred where fire in the belly had to be prized above stock in munitions. Unmarried pilots especially found their first Blighty leave so demoralising that thereafter many opted to stay in Paris; an act rarely popular when the Mess awaited José Collins' latest record. But COs respected the wisdom of such decisions.

In the steamy air of June 23 12 FE 2bs set their pulpits at Metz. B5625 was piloted by a New Zealand artist, Lieut A. R. Kingsford, who tried to deceive the guns by swinging into the town from the north. The ruse worked until he was between Metz and the *flak*-stuffed Forêt de Remilly. Then a triangle of searchlights, lately placed to catch clever fellows, whipped out and a shell burst under the left wing.

The observer, Lieut S. N. Bourne of Canterbury, yelled that he wanted to use his Lewis, but Kingsford was too busy weaving the suddenly floppy machine. He shook off two beams but plunged 5300 ft down the bright tunnel of the other without upsetting the operator.

Any second now a machine gun must drill into them . . . Despairingly Bourne tugged the bomb release. It stuck. Again he pulled, and the searchlight's bluey-white glare dissolved in a whorl of yellow flame.

Weak all through, Kingsford straightened out and flew groggily north until it dawned on him that Thionville, nearly 20 miles distant, was blacking out in agitation. Swallowing their fright the lonely couple returned to their duty, entering Metz at 4000 ft. Gliding down they let go four 25-pounders to the left of the main lines, where the other Fees had wrecked Track 86 and damaged a train. Instantly searchlights began their darting, but Kingsford dodged them easily until Bourne was ready to drop the 230-pounder and a trio of 25s in the left rack. Three blasts followed, and almost certainly these were the explosions which smashed a railway workshop at 12.30 am.

The red eyes of AA pierced the night, but another peril alarmed Bourne as the old 'pusher' churned homewards.

Out under the left wing there was a lighter patch—the 25 lb HE bomb which should have made an uncounted flash at Metz. Bourne yanked feverishly at the slack toggle but without response. The landing jar might—just might—loosen the live explosive and bowl it into nearby ground crew or aeroplanes. In the chill darkness, at an hour when the human spirit is presumed to be at its lowest, Bourne made his decision.

Shouting the trouble into Kingsford's ear he asked him to hold the machine steady. Then, gripping the pilot's coaming he eased his right leg past the protruding elevator rocker-bar, wiggling his toes into the foothole at the bottom of the nacelle. With Kingsford countering the Fee's urge to rear away into a roll he quit the cockpit, hanging in space until he could grasp an interplane strut and stretch his foot to the wing. Transferring his leather-swaddled bulk he wormed belly down alongside the hot clanking engine.

Bourne was now ensconced amid a web of wires. If one snagged his goggles or the straps of his leather coat billowing in the 70 mph wind it could twitch him into the void. Yet he managed to progress four feet, spreadeagling himself towards the leading edge and keeping his knees on the wing ribs to avoid breaking through the fabric.

Locking a foot and an arm in the wires he leaned into the blackness. His gauntletted fingers fiddled blindly with the bomb clasps. Something gave—and Kingsford immediately countered the upsurging wing while Bourne clung on with every fibre of muscle. It was done; all but the equally agonising crawl back.

They landed uneventfully, and there was a corollary understood by other flyers who smiled wryly over so many awards that 'came up with the rations'. Bourne made Kingsford promise not to mention what had taken place.

Forty hours passed and Bourne and Kingsford returned with a spluttering Beardmore after trying for Boulay aerodrome, 50 miles north-west of Lighthouse C. When again ready to catch up with 14 luckier crews they heard the unsynchronised *pour vous-pour vous* of Hun engines and the whistle of four descending missiles. Hurriedly the flarepath was doused and through bomb fumes FE 5625 raced off without its benefit.

Four storage sheds were well alight when she reached Boulay and turning to line up a 230-pounder with other buildings Kingsford was snared by a *scheinenwerfer* and its consorting machine guns. Quickly he dropped a parachute flare and the searchlight sidestepped to pursue it.

A few minutes from Boulay Bourne spotted landing lights, and they circled until a twin-engined Hun—probably the one that had interrupted their departure from Ochey—rolled his wheels. As ground staff ran towards it the Fee dived to 600 ft and Bourne distributed a 97-round Lewis drum into the tableau. Out went the lights.

This marked the end of happiness for the Boulay airmen. Within two days another of their Gothas was set alight by 100 Sqn, and they sought a nest at Friesdorf aerodrome. Bombed there, too, they fled to Lillingen where the soil was always soggy. The IF trailed them; and at Ruplingen, the final choice, landing was so dangerous they became virtually grounded.

If bombers could be subdued the *Kests* could not, as a massed force learned during their June 26 sortie to Karlsruhe. Many EA went for 104 Sqn, four of whose pilots had failed to rendezvous—one falling victim to *Vfw* Willy Rössel at Offenburg and the other wandering across the border until encouraged to land by Swiss AA fire. Seeing the new boys' plight 99 Sqn, minus five aircraft through conked motors and a fainted observer, attempted to formate with them. But climbing speeds and tactical ideas were different and the confused link-up benefited the Huns. The other unit, 55, carried out its usual well-co-ordinated operation for the cost of one crew driven down at Saarbrücken by *Vfw* Heidseld.

Evidently Wing HQ thought big combinations, however ill-assorted, were at worst a psychological barrier to the interceptors, for next day a similar mission was flown to Thionville with 55 Sqn in top station. The pilots of 12 Albatros, Fokker triplanes, and Pfalz which snarled in at point-blank range were brave men. Shooting by 99 Sqn observers was particularly steady and accurate, one scout disintegrating and littering the sky with its gaudy fabric. A bullet pierced Lieut H. Sanders' leg but, coolly allowing for the wobbliness of his platform the gunner, 2nd Lieut W. B. Walker, sent the culprit down in flames and won the DFC.

Luck was better than skill. Grounded after his mid-air faint on the way to Karlsruhe, 2nd Lieut B. S. W. Taylor was upset that his pilot, 2nd Lieut E. A. Chapin, had to replace him. Over Thionville Chapin's machine fell blazing.

Mist stopped a strafe on Frescaty aerodrome the following eve; but not a German intruder who espied movement on the very white road between Toul and Ochey. His tracers sparked around the American staff car in which Colonel T. D. Milling, Mitchell's training officer, and Major Hall, operations aide, were taking home their dinner guests, Lieut-Colonel Baldwin and Lieut-Colonel J. H. A. Landon, from July 1 to command the

IF's new 83rd Wing. Its offside rear wheel punctured, the vehicle slithered to the bottom of a hill. Rather ruffled, they climbed out to inspect the damage. Someone struck a match.

That was all the EA needed. Banking sharply it jettisoned two bombs, one exploding in a ditch 10 ft from the group. Baldwin crumpled with a torn knee, Landon with a gashed head, the chauffeur with mortal wounds.

This incident hardened Trenchard's resolve to keep his air free of the night bugs, but squadron casualty returns were daunting. The DH 9s were proving impossible, although 104 Sqn shaped more promisingly in a prolonged fight in and out of Landau on June 30, two Huns being crashed and two others driven down for the loss of a Nine which was *Vfw* Krüger's second victory.

Major Pattinson reported that No. 99 was much below strength and that his problem was to bring on new pilots quickly as the casualties, both sick and wounded, had far outrun the effective reinforcements.

Trenchard explained the statistics to Weir. It took, he said, at least five days for replacement pilots to travel from England after which they spent a fortnight practising formation work—otherwise collisions would be prohibitive. Leave, imperative if they were to keep fit, removed two pilots at any time. Probably two more would be sick, which definition included nervous breakdowns. Twenty-one pilots 'on establishment' normally amounted to under 12. And he blamed himself for not giving sufficient warning that his losses would average one aircraft out of 12 on every mission: although in doing so he must have forgotten his complaints about the quality of Nines.

Weir, in his turn, was discouraging about future supplies of Nines, Salmond's units also having experienced an abnormal number of crashes through the inability of virgin pilots to cope with the Puma's quirks.

Nevertheless, the Air Ministry's fresh and grossly inflated expansion programme for the IF envisaged 60 bomber squadrons by the end of September—40 based in France, 20 in Britain. More would be heard of the Homeland contingent. But, wisely, the plan was marked 'provisional'.

# PHASE III

## *'The German is susceptible to bloodiness . . .'*

# 6 *'There shall the vultures also be gathered, every one with her mate.' (Isaiah 34:15)*

Knowing their difficulties in facing the veteran *Jagdgeschwadern* (hunting groups) I, II, and III on the St Mihiel sector where the French Sixth Army had been decimated, Trenchard was loath to shift part of his burden to the Americans. After dropping more bombs during May than the total for the previous six months, in June the strategic squadrons had again raised the figure—to 70 tons, at the cost of only nine 'missing' machines. That ratio, however, was unlikely to continue when the *Kests* formed a barrier to the targets instead of challenging around the objective or along the bombers' return route.

So the General told Mitchell that enemy spotters were beginning to plot the bombers' outward courses and direct the requisite number of interceptors into their path. He asked for protection in the initial stage, especially over the Lines, from the 1st Pursuit Group, whose redoubtable pilots included Eddie Rickenbacker, Reed M. Chambers, and Sumner Sewell.

This aid, willingly afforded, was some comfort; although in dim visibility it promoted a few embarrassing incidents since the exposed engines of DH 9s gave them a 'Hunnish' appearance and IF gunners, unaccustomed to friendly fighters, were quick on the trigger.

Self-help was an axiom of John Baldwin. When a Sandhurst cadet in 1910 he had risked expulsion to earn enough as a spare-time Brooklands mechanic to be taught 'pilotage', which, next to riding horses, was what he liked best about life. If ever a commander flew every 41st Wing mission vicariously it was Baldwin. He could not be content with casual help, and devised a scheme to complement the American cover. An hour or so prior to a main force taking off, a section of bombers manned largely by replacements trailed their coats over a different sector. While receiving a baptism in combat tactics the newcomers drew off a portion of the opposition.

This 'decoy' worked first on July 2 when Trier, Conz, and Metz were assaulted, although its benefit was nullified for 104 Sqn by a succession of forced-landings which reduced the formation to four aircraft. Trenchard's greatest fear was for this suffering unit, whose immaturity was painfully exposed on the 5th. Near Blamont, a quarter of the way to their goal of Kaiserslautern, the leader's Puma gave out and he dumped his bombs. Utterly confused the rest followed suit and mangled the innocent village of Barbas.

Around this hour Thom was tangling with eight Huns near Saarbrücken. Tracers ripped through fabric, killing his gunner, 2nd Lieut L. G. Claye, and bruising his own arm. Nobody dropped out and Lewis fire stripped the wings from one scout and got his companion in a fast spin. The leader's Nine was so shot about that it had to be rebuilt.

Within 48 hours he was out again, at Kaiserslautern, with Taylor as deputy and a flight of 104 Sqn on his flank. The Puma showed its teeth as usual and at an impossible moment for Taylor, who crunched into a cornfield and wrote-off the machine. The rest made up for that by bashing the railway and station buildings. There was the customary scrap with eight Huns, who spent most of their fury on '104' and lost one of their number. For his steadiness in this and similar predicaments Lieut W. G. Stevenson received the DFC.

In the pugnacious tradition of the de Havilland squadrons Taylor, although bruised and shaken, led six aircraft to Bühl aerodrome the next afternoon. The biggest permanent hangar was demolished and bomb pits were dug in the tarmac fronting several others. That night Azelot was bombed for the first time, two drivers being wounded.

From the 8th to the 15th flying was difficult enough for skilled officers, mists, eight-tenths cloud, and boisterous winds alternating to fray taut nerves. But during the frequent stand-downs a timely panacea was applied through simple amusements.

There were a few inter-unit football and medicine ball matches but each squadron catered for its own needs. Night bombers automatically profited from the change in their topsy-turvy operational routine which required tea and a sandwich to be taken in bed at 9 am, breakfast at 11.30 am, dinner at 4.30 pm, and supper at 10.30 pm. Their outdoor pursuits differed little from those of the de Havilland men. These were rugged; and none more so than in 55 Sqn whose members came from every province of Canada, Australia, New Zealand, India, Ceylon, South Africa, Malay States, Falkland Islands, Egypt, Spain, and Switzerland, besides the British Isles and the United States.

The quietest of their excursions was fuel foraging in the woods, exercise wholly approved by a dog named Roger who in a less tranquil moment had been scooped up by a nimble observer jumping from and back into a DH 4 as it blandly taxied past the hangars of 100 Sqn, his erstwhile owners.

Still, the woods held their excitements, as an FE pilot remarked when to evade a strafing Hun he dashed into the brush—and came out faster, encouraged by a wild boar.

On rain-lashed nights the fug of the Mess anteroom was more welcome than the delights of Nancy, guests frequently being attracted to 100's huge brazier, whose four open sides could 'toast' innumerable officers while the phonograph scratched a protest against Continental mandolins and a well-liquored piano.

Among walls the sporting prints which vied with cut-outs from *La Vie Parisienne* were bequests from long-gone Regulars—who would have stiffened at the 'shop' talk indulged by the Cinderella Service, at the flippant vocabulary of 'committing crashery' on aeroplanes, dropping 'pills' and 'eggs', 'fanning down' targets, deriding the fervour of 'split arse merchants' and 'hot stuffers' and 'kiwis' (ground officers) who got into 'a flat spin' over trifles.

Amenities of the sort Bomber Command one day could employ were inconceivable, even the electricity supply being supplemented by the traditional 'Dawn Patrol' candles in bottles in case a battery failed suddenly. Not until winter would Charlie Chaplin flicker on a roller screen at Xaffévillers, and bands were subject to the discord of postings. But few sports sustained morale better than Tanks—with upturned sofas for obstacles, sofa siphons for guns—and COs did not worry so long as an officer could still walk along the ceiling when hoisted by his raucous friends.

German civilians, too, were glad of the lull but exploited it less lightheartedly.

Kaiserslautern, for example, where the architecture of the

Gross armature works, Jalna's brewery, and Eckel's furniture stores had been violently rearranged, spent the time in restoring gas and water systems disrupted in the Krimm district on July 7. As a citizen recorded, 'one can no longer walk about; there is so much glass . . . *Fräulein Flieger* is with us night and day. It is simply a terrible life for us.'

The heart cries echoed through Coblenz, Saarbrücken, Thionville, Offenburg, Saarburg, Mannheim, and Luxembourg during the first half of the month; and on July 12 progress was summed up for Trenchard by Air Intelligence:

'The panic created at Cologne, especially, was intense and if we had only continued these bombing expeditions *for a few days consecutively* the result would have surpassed expectations. Those of our Dutch friends who take an interest in our winning the war are more than puzzled at the fact that our raids are not *more continuous and more powerful.*

'. . . It is the one form of punishment which the civil population cannot stand. Police regulations or no police regulations, the fact remains that after each raid there has been a very nasty moment for the authorities. If these raids were sufficiently continuous the amount of dissatisfaction and panic would be such that great events might follow.'

A freelance Swiss agent reinforced this report by declaring, 'if the Allies had their wits about them they would not stop bombing Germany for an hour. The population is so demoralised that no victories can counter-balance the effect.'

In AI files this man was classed as 'pro-German'; and if his evidence was not encouraging enough on the 18th a Dutch traveller found the Rhine population 'nervous, depressed, and (they think it) better to discuss peace terms at once than to expose women to such risks'.

Women were not the IF's quarry, nor did German military Staff think so. Coughing through the constantly stirred smoke of Metz, so situated that weather-frustrated crews used it as a bomb alley, they did not divine, or particularly care, that the town's total dead would amount to 132, its wounded to 300. They were just tired of twisted tracks, pulverised rolling stock, and stalled supply trains. At some time every line in the Triangle had been repaired. Since the Schlieffen Plan of the Nineties the German military machine had run on steel wheels and now its momentum was slowing.

A partial solution came with the formation of *Eisenbahn Truppen* (railway platoons), responsible for clearing wreckage and restoring traffic flow. Metz, Thionville, Coblenz, and Cologne were their chief charges, but counter-measures were promulgated throughout the beset territories. Unless trains quit a main station within 10 minutes they were shunted into sidings; air raid 'alerts' halted all except troop and express trains; and lights at stations and signal boxes were screened or extinguished.

While these precautions checked the rot at pivotal points inevitably their repercussions rippled over the entire railway system and enhanced the IF's impression.

The strain on railway personnel grew severe. To avoid mistakes in communication technical staff were denied their customary 'reliefs'. Off-duty employees supplemented the *Eisenbahn Truppen* in building special branch lines for traffic re-routing. Signalmen caused accidents when they failed to grasp frequent and complicated alterations in switching plans. Movement by night was perilous and restricted.

Any benefits of such activity did not affect Thionville station on July 16 when, diverted from Stuttgart by thunder-storms, 99 Sqn essayed the most destructive jaunt of its career. Thom and Beecroft headed 12 crews into a strong west wind, with 55 Sqn backing up. Twenty bombs swished into the goods loading area and set off stacks of loose shells and hand grenades. Two hit a munitions train, detonating 15 trucks. Recklessly valiant railwaymen unhooked 25 wagons and towed them through the inferno. The dumb neutrality of 60 horses perished with them in adjacent rolling stock also carrying medical supplies, and surrounding buildings crumbled under a shroud of black and beige smoke.

To observers 20 miles away the incandescent reflection on the clouds was awesome even in the sunlight.

Paint bubbling in the intense heat, one train puffed out of its layby as the drone of the intact raiders died away. It was packed with British prisoners who noted 10 locomotives on their sides with a mass of coach debris snaking behind them. Water towers were crushed and water mains spouting. Because 400 *Eisenbahn Truppen* spent the next 48 hours with lifting gear and picks to clear a mainline passage that train wandered to Longuyon and Audun-le-Roman before crawling, short of coal, into Metz.

The Thionville public took to the shelters at 2 pm and few

ventured out until 10 o'clock. Ten of them were killed compared with 83 soldiers but the moral effect of their experience was prodigious, and months later town officials said none would ever forget the date.

A 35 mph wind at 12,000 ft, allied with overheated Pumas and heavy AA fire, nullified No. 99's attempt to repeat the performance in the morning. Six aircraft, half the starters, reached the town and smacked 10 bombs on to the smouldering ruins.

No doubt Trenchard's 'reliable sources' were right to predict a collapse of German morale had this type of battering been maintained, but not since June 29/30 at Mannheim had a round-the-clock strike been feasible. In seizing the initiative, which it would never lose, on aerodrome strafes the IF had had to neglect its strategic purpose. Lately, industrial targets for 100 Sqn and 216 Sqn had been fewer, but to prepare them or investigate results 55 Sqn alone undertook nine photo reconnaissances over Hun aerodromes that month.

The tanning being administered as a consequence to the German aerodromes alone justified the extra tension. Just the same a few EA took off between the bomb holes and made '104' pay with the destruction of their transport and '99' with more wounded ground staff. Amazingly, the hangars escaped.

Alongside these hindrances Trenchard evaluated the latest news from the Chief of Air Staff. Besides the 60 'paper' night-bombing outfits earmarked for the Force, Sykes promised 44 day squadrons, 20 of them support-fighters. The IF commander bluntly told Weir that this was fantasy. No truly long-range escorts had been tested and he would not be saddled with standard single-seaters. In any case, the total figure was beyond attainment, and grudgingly he agreed to a pruned total estimate of 54 squadrons. Five reached him before Cease Fire.

Were these events not aggravating enough, coincidentally Trenchard exchanged views with the Americans on the initiation and composition of the proposed joint command. He volunteered to train mechanics and service American aircraft—'for accounting purposes three DH 4s or DH 9s shall be equivalent to one Handley Page'—at his Courbon depot.

'Bombardment' aircrews would be instructed operationally with IF units, the culmination being the formation of their own squadrons prior to Anglo-American fusion.

Trenchard believed deeply and selflessly in the future of this project, urging Weir to allot HPs and FEs to home-based RAF schools where American cadets were congregating, irrespective of this temporarily lessening his own meagre supply.

The value of British experience was not lost on Billy Mitchell, within weeks of becoming General Commanding the US First Army's Air Service. On July 10 his 96th Aero Sqn had received a salutary lesson when the CO, Major Harry M. Brown, had staged a strategic mission with six Breguet 14B–2s in rain and under a low ceiling. Having hauled above the clouds the flight lost its bearings, eventually descending through a 'hole' over a city which the lead observer, Lieut Hal McChesney, thought might be German. Brown disagreeed and all of them landed. They were at Coblenz, about 90 miles NE of their objective, Conflans. And guests of the Kaiser . . .

A Rumpler-borne message that fluttered to Mitchell read, cheekily: 'We thank you for the fine aeroplanes and equipment which you have sent us, but what shall we do with the Major?'

Mitchell thought the benighted Major was far safer where he was.

The IF was equally pleased with its incoming 'Yanks' who introduced poker to the Mess anteroom and filled the warm evenings with the nostalgic twang of ukeleles and Hawaiian melodies. 'Great appreciation, both as pilots and comrades . . .' was the verdict of 55 Sqn, which was also favourably disposed towards the first American-built DH 4, No. 32077, to arrive at Azelot. A product of the Dayton-Wright Corpn of Ohio it was pulled by a 400 hp Liberty engine which made it nose heavy.

The story of the Liberty's birth was pure Americana, a sample of what the Kaiser shipyards would accomplish with the Liberty ships of another war. A mass-production engine being essential, a conference lasting from the afternoon of June 3, 1917, until 2.30 am on June 4 was called; and two engineers spent the next five days in a Washington hotel working alternate 24-hour shifts. The engine was completed in 12 factories between Connecticut and California, and was delivered to Washington on Independence Day—a month and a day from the time of asking. It was flown on August 20.

A V-type, water-cooled, motor, the Liberty 12 employed a high tension coil instead of magnetos and Britain, disturbed by the diminution of Rolls-Royce turnover, placed an order for 3000 by the following January, deliveries to start with 500.

But the country was not geared to astronomical demands and by the end of March the purchaser had received 10 and in July the flow dried up at 620—to the vexation of Winston Churchill, who discovered that the US Navy had claimed priority.

Bitterly he said: 'A great part of these precious engines on which the whole of our offensive bombing programme depends has up to date been swallowed up by American aviation.'

Actually, the Tank Corps was after Libertys, too; and the best Churchill's complaints could elicit was a promise that 4560 engines would be provided during 1919. That might have been feasible, for in October 4200 came off the fantastic assembly lines.

The Liberty owned by 55 Sqn was in an aircraft that had been put together from early British drawings, and the undercart was located too far aft. Consequently it tended to tip up in the soggy soil of French fields. Air performance was fine, and the American nickname for it of 'Flaming Coffin' was a slander to which hardened flyers did not subscribe.

Twelve conventional Fours were airborne at 5 am on July 20, with flight leaders 'Billy' Williams and Lieut P. E. Welchman pointing them for the Mercedes aero engine works in the Untertürkheim suburb of Stuttgart. As they crossed the Lines at 14,000 ft the snow-topped Swiss Alps glittered far to starboard. An hour passed and the dark mass of Strasbourg loomed under the blunt noses. Marking it were black *flak* paths; but these could be skirted, whereas a lurking frontal wind made Williams recollect fuel consumption and alter course across the Black Forest to Oberndorf.

On to the Mauser small arms works and railway sidings the '55' pilots rained their loads, and then sighted 15 Albatros D5s of *Kest* 4B coming in from Freiburg at 17,000 ft.

Sgt F. E. Nash noted that his observer, Sgt W. E. Baker, had slipped home the rear joystick in case the pilot were knocked out; and the scrap started. Out at left flank Lieut Christopher Young's machine rolled over, an orange and black plume unfurling from its riven main tank. Baker swivelled the Scarff ring, pumping tracer into the victorious Albatros which flipped into a spin with flames swathing the belly. Then, with a stunning bang, water and steam gushed over Nash's thighs. Bullets gouged holes around him and jerking a frantic glance over his shoulder he was dismayed by the twin Lewises pointing straight up and unattended. He smelt petrol, and at that instant was sledgehammered in the back.

The siren call of tortured wires drew him to consciousness and through a grey veil he perceived the speed was nearly off the clock at 180 mph and the altimeter winding down to 7000 ft. Willing a flabby left arm to close the throttle he eased on the control column. No response.

Nash now knew. Baker's dead weight was pressed on to the emergency stick, locking the elevators; the observer's life-preserver turned into his pilot's killer.

Half-rising in his harness Nash put his waning strength on to the lever, braced his feet against the rudder bar, and heaved—realising as he did so that if he won the wings were bound to rip off. Again and again he strained. The stick creaked back; the horizon slid on to the windshield; and the stout old de Havilland somehow held together. But too much height had been lost. The only route open was down.

The cockpit was a shambles, even the petrol pipe to the underseat tank hanging in two pieces, and Nash could see only one possible field—stamp-sized and bordered by fir trees. Sideslipping he straightened late, hit a ridge, and wiped off the undercarriage before pancaking from 15 ft.

The time was 8.25 am. With blood seeping from bullet holes in his shoulder and a chunk of the main tank protruding from his back Nash sought to lift down his observer's body so that he might burn the machine. As he struggled an Albatros S-turned tightly down and bounced across to him.

Smoking the *Kest* pilot's cigarettes he was taken to hospital, at whose doors a civilian mob howled for his head. Staff placed him in the cellars, a convenient shelter next day when No. 55 blew up 200 tons of explosives at the nearby Rottweil factories, whose plight could be seen written in smoke pillars from 60 miles away.

The Germans credited *Vfw* Heppner and *Uffz* Pohlmann with their first victories at Oberndorf and mourned three Messmates, two of them fallen to Welchman's front Vickers and to Lieut Keep's gunner, 2nd Lieut J. S. Pollock. A fortnight passed before the remains of Young's observer, Lieut R. A. Butler—who jumped to escape burning—were uncovered in a clump of fir trees. Two days after the Armistice Mrs Young of Streatham was still advertising for information about her equally unfortunate husband.

For companions in misfortune Nash had two Azelot aviators, 2nd Lieut F. G. Thompson and his observer, 2nd Lieut S. C. Thornley, whose DH 9 had first been driven off Stuttgart by the wind and then assailed by EA which holed the radiator. As they recrossed the Rhine the engine stopped. But they had made a mess at Offenburg.

Wilful westerly currents banded against 55 and 99 Sqns on July 22, and the Nines again abandoned Stuttgart. Twelve laid neat rows of blossoms across the railway sidings and station, felling a bridge *en route* but overshooting slightly into the town itself. Bombs gone, they were involved in a ruckus with 16 Albatros and Pfalz, one of which blundered into cross-fire from Lieut L. V. Dennis and Sgt F. L. Lee and hurtled down with blazing tanks.

More radiators attracted bullets and Captain Thom, noticing the white stream left by 2nd Lieut G. Broadbent, dived repeatedly, snapping Vickers bursts at hungry Huns and clinging to the crippled machine as it staggered round the Vosges foothills.

Broadbent and observer Sgt J. Jones touched down in a narrow valley with only slight damage to the undercarriage. Not sure of the location they sprinted for cover and were cowering in undergrowth when they heard a disgruntled voice call, 'Where have those goddamed aviators gone?' They were at Raon l'Étape on the borderline, and surrounded by American doughboys.

Lieut F. Smith was in worse distress, bullets snipping his fuselage the moment his observer, Sgt F. Coulsen, became disabled with an arm wound, without cover, and with an engine fast seizing up. Far behind the hard-pressed formation he was driven so low that his wheels brushed hillocks as he crossed them with the Nine shuddering on the verge of a stall. Either scared by the proximity of the ground or satisfied that he must crash, the Huns pulled away.

Smith, three weeks with the squadron, had coaxed just enough power to reach Raon l'Étape when a slightly steeper hill beat him. It was studded with fir trees and though by dabs on the rudder he eluded their trunks he could not pass the spearing branches.

Fabric scaled off in a leafy storm as he fought to keep some air flowing over the control surfaces. The wheels bounced, there came a sharp crack from the undercarriage, and the crew were gripped in the vice of their safety harness.

The Country: Smoke rising from Brebach works, Saarbrücken, on 7 September, 1918. Photographed by 55 Sqn. at f.8¼.

Cargo: Bombing-up FE 2B with 112-pounders. Coopers under wings. Crew wearing Sidcots.

Carrier: A 852, the FE which hit balloon barrage, warming up at end of flare-path.

'Closing Up': DH9As bunching against Fokker Triplanes and Fokker D 7s. Triplane in foreground has obsolete paté crosses. (*Painting by G. Horace Davis, 1919.*)

The Straggler (*1918 painting by Joseph Simpson*): DH9, with radiator down, fights off Albatros D 5s.

A Deep Breath . . . Flight Sgt adjusts oxygen mask. Observe petrol pump vanes between DH 4 cockpits

. . . but Cold Feet? Electrical heating extended only to crew's trunks and arms.

*Above left.* The High: H-P observer with Scarff-mounted Lewis, bomb sight, and pitot tube—registering airspeed—in front of trapdoor under nose.

*Above right.* The Mighty: 0/100 ready for action. Bomb sight is under pilot's feet. Rear Lewises on individual pillars.

The Fallen: H-P down in Hunland. Bomb cells exposed above near wheels. V-aperture was for belly gun.

The 'Offices': Very cartridges at bottom of H-P pilot's windscreen. Canvas bag on Lewis caught expelled cartridge cases.

DH9A. *Dials l to r, top:* oil temp., clock, fuel cock, R.P.M. *Centre:* oil pressure, fuel gauge, primer pump, cross-level, A.S.I., altimeter. *Bottom:* Very light holder, Creagh-Osborne 5/17 compass, Liberty ammeter.

*Top*. Ours: Fitting the Liberty 12.

*Centre*. Theirs: Pfalz D 3.

*Below:* SS D 3. Note hole in wheel cover.

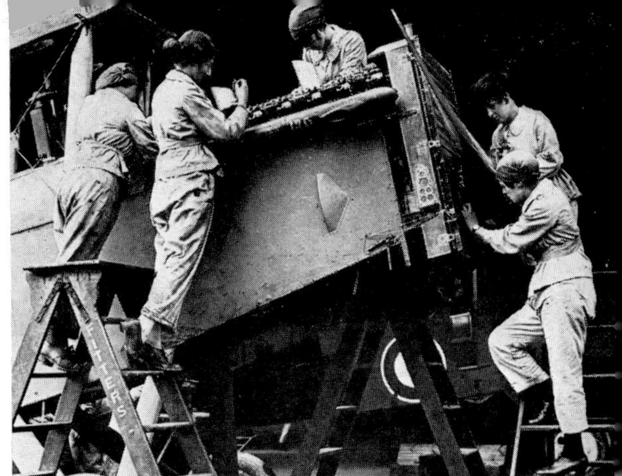

*War*: HP V/1500 wearing experimental night bomber roundels—white, red, blue from outer ring.

*Peace*: Mail Run. DH9A at Maisoncelle, winter of 1918. No. 1004 flown by Captain William Armstrong, AFC.

The engine bearers had snapped and the Puma was buried in the soft earth. Linen strips drooped from the wings like the skin of a moulting animal. Where the fuselage had not been skeletonised twigs stuck out as impertinently as banderillas in a bull. By the grace of Smith's grit and airmanship the Nine had flown —ploughed would be more apt—through half a wood. But its occupants were on the right side, and to them that was all that mattered.

Stuttgart certainly was the jinx trip. Not since March had any day flyer beaten the sly winds, and the alternative targets of Baden-Baden, Offenburg, and Oberndorf were being 'fanned down' regularly, No. 99 having a typically sticky time on July 30.

In low spirits because of its recalcitrant engines, the squadron was employing two spare machines—whose crews would otherwise have been resting—to accompany the duty flights during the climb across the Lines. If all went as planned they could return to their truckle beds. This time six of the 12 dropped out, disabled by oil leaks, cracked cylinders, and any other ill to which Puma drivers fell heir. Thick mist rolled up east of the Vosges and, losing contact, one machine flew unwittingly south to Dijon. Forgetting Stuttgart and sweating out the collision risk his companions bombed Lahr without hope of cofirming hits.

Unloaded, the Nines could just make 85 mph at 13,000 ft and as they recrossed the Rhine 20 Huns overhauled them and took swift toll of the fledglings. American Philip Dietz, a '104' officer with '99' for a fortnight, and his passenger, 2nd Lieut C. W. Batty (joined July 3), were killed when *Oblt* Muhlfeld's repeated Maxim bursts tore their machine apart. Radiator steaming and a gaping hole in his foot, 2nd Lieut G. Martin (June 30) steered his aeroplane gently into a marsh in the futile bid to save his dying gunner. An old hand, Lieut H. S. Notley, set one Hun alight. Sgt Lee (June 30), a fabulous sharpshooter, cut through the cockpit of another, whose occupant fell in the hideous parody of a balancing act which was the rarest but most traumatic sight in a dogfight. That was his third victory and brought the immediate award of the DFM. Brian Taylor avenged his late pilot with an Albatros which shed its wings in a vicious spin. He received the DFC for that feat, and efforts on 19 successful raids before his fainting spell.

The balance sheet could have been worse, for in this cruel

adventure fledglings were deductible expenses. But the *Kests* were not content with the soft core.

Mainz was the objective for 12 of the squadron under Captain Taylor and Lieut E. L. Doidge the next day. Three turned back with faltering motors before Saarburg, but the formation closed tightly in time to meet the 40 black-crossed scouts which scurried from the eyries of *Kest* 3 at Morhange and *Kest* 2 at Saarbrücken.

The customary rush did not come. Calmly the enemy spread out into the Western Front *kettes* (chains) of three and four, leaving six freelances wheeling like vultures against the sun. When at last the chains lashed out, each in turn sought one victim. There was to be no respite and as the red tracer sparks and jazzy smoke trails curled about them '99' expected they would be lucky to see Azelot let alone Mainz. Five managed to toggle into the railway station of Saarbrücken.

Even the heat conspired to their ruin, for they lowered radiators to cool gasping engines and coming from underneath or behind the EA found the vulnerable area increased by one-third. All the skill of seasoned bomber men did not prevail. Five officers died, seven were captured.

Two Nines, fit for kindling, got back thanks to cover from 104 Sqn who reached the scene opportunely. From one stepped Taylor, who reported: 'We also accounted for eight enemy scouts definitely known to have crashed . . . I recommend that we return and finish the job.'

As triumphs can be reckoned in such disparate warfare this was a memorable one, removing eight of the squadron's 'originals' and lacerating the morale of the recent arrivals. Trenchard, upset as he had not been since Bloody April, motored at once to the dazed unit. Baring, for three years his shadow on visits of this nature, heard him tell the haggard youngsters that 'where we had the advantage over the enemy was that our spirit was such that we could face and get over our losses and go on in spite of them, and that the enemy couldn't'.

Resilient words, even from this tough, patently sincere, old-young man could not overcome the physical facts. Pattinson closed down the squadron until he felt the rushed replacements—formation experience nil, map reading skimped—had half a chance of surviving their first 'show'.

The General notified Weir of the setback, and reminded him that the IF was also fighting the elements. One squadron Cologne-bound had the wind change on them at Coblenz, five hours out, and near the Lines ran out of petrol. This forced them to glide down through hills, a situation that had badly scared them. Night raids on Stuttgart had been more satisfactory but '. . . the Handley Pages got there by dint of pressure, pressure, pressure . . .'

The record distance for this, the first full month of IF operations, was 272 miles by day, 300 by night, the flying hours amounting to 1768 during daylight and 767 at night.

Appropriately the August sun brought the hum of hornets and wasps above the ripening wheat and plump white raspberries framing the Nancy group of aerodromes and, more hearteningly still, renewed execration from German townships. On the 1st 55 Sqn toggled above Düren putting, as the Mayor said, 'the population into great consternation'. Understandably, as there were 26 casualties, 12 dead, in two elementary schools, post office, and houses. Few of the 28 bombs disturbed the factories, cloud and wind having put off the aimers.

Less worthy of support was the eruption at Trier, which between July 1 and August 9 received three visitations. On the 7th the chief *bürgermeister* shouted to a full session of the council:

'We, as a city which has been the specially selected target, finally demand a definite statement that there does exist a legal claim to compensate for damage. This cannot reasonably be postponed any longer.'

His solicitude for property owners was abetted by the *Trierische Landeszeitung*. 'How often, and particularly here, has this unpleasant topic arisen without any result! When East Prussia was suffering from the Russian invasion efforts were speedily made to come to the assistance of the unfortunate province. The whole of Germany, and not least the Rhine province, did all it could to repair the damage . . . A milliard Marks[1] were readily placed at the disposal of shipowners for the building of their fleet. Heaven knows when the money will be used. We unfortunate Rhinelanders [are] under the constant threat of attack interrupted only by a friendly spell of rain.

'Either: let it be seen that the criminal barbarity of these aerial attacks on the defenceless civilian population ceases once and for all; or: let the Government state that we can recover

1. £50,000,000.

for all damage and (which is the main thing) damage to life and limb.'

Not since the 1870 war had the thread-thin unity of the German states been more contemptuously displayed. Nor was the journal's detestation of the Prussian Junkers yet spent:

'Some time ago, mark you, a [Reichstag] member stated in the House that "we could not be the first to offer to come to an understanding". As mere subjects we ask: "Why not, pray? We are surely winning?"

'But if they cannot, have they on the other side of the Elbe a clear conception of the facts? If not, we suggest some of our leading politicians come and live for a time in Trier!'

What a spate, from a town which in the whole of 1918 would have seven citizens killed and 12 wounded...

The same day 104 Sqn lost a machine but claimed three EA out of control in a running battle over Karlsruhe. Bombs were quickly jettisoned and the leader feared one 'stick' had struck the big POW camp. As though by telepathy the Wolff Agency, in the hope of scaring off future raiders, announced this was so.

Within hours Air Intelligence scotched the lie, submitting an agent's gleanings fantastic in their scrupulous detail. For example: '. . . Central station, 11 bombs. Two in tunnel; one on Platform 4, wrecking parts of express train from Offenburg; one on lines and goods truck; one in passage near steps leading to Platform 9; two on lines by Platform 6A; two outside west entrance; one in the Maxan station (considerable damage in express goods room); one close to east wing of station.' Not all the heroes behind IF operations were privileged to work in the clean air or to die with dignity among comrades.

In London, however, where strikes were depriving the RAF of aircraft and spares, the various perils of Siege By Air were rarely appreciated. It took a C. G. Grey, Editor of *The Aeroplane*, to abuse the slacking workers of Coventry and to prophesy that one day their city would learn what bombing meant. The lay Press contented itself with asking why Frankfurt-am-Main was not on the target list. Indeed *Flight* joined the chorus with its suspicions of political intrigue. The city, it conjectured, was not inhabited by a gentler race of Hun deserving to be spared. Instead it was the HQ of cosmopolitan finance, and '. . . a city where there are many interests shared by the financial groups of aliens who give us the doubtful benefit of their presence here. [They] have an all too large number of friends in high places . . .'

The military truth was that to attack Prussia's banking centre, ironically the birthplace of Goethe, a bomber would fly half the length of Britain and brave a hinterland more heavily guarded than any experienced before. En route the aeroplane would pass between Sarreburg and Strasbourg, Pirmasens and Karlsruhe, Kaiserslautern and Mannheim, and near to Saarbrücken, every one a region of maximum danger. By day the *Kests* could be expected to exsanguinate the biggest force that could be scraped together.

So in setting off at 5.20 am on August 12 '55' was trying to break Germany's bank the hardest way. *Flak* batteries peppered their tails from Badonviller, an enormous investment without profit. Surprisingly, interceptors were also eluded and at eight o'clock, still in two compact flights, they emptied their racks. Bursts were all within a circle 1000 metres in diameter, mature aiming from 14,000 ft had the direction been right.

As it was the clusters overshot into civil property of the West End, especially in the Bockenheim Landstrasse, which bore the brunt. Sixteen people were killed, 26 injured, and the Kaiser's message of sympathy over 'this attack contrary to International Law' did not stem a stream of rich evacuees.

Coolly an American pilot, 2nd Lieut Don J. Waterous, took eight photographs before the DH 4s turned south, a move interrupted west of Mannheim by 35 Fokker D7s, Albatros, and the nasty new Siemens Schuckerts. Pugnaciously '55' demonstrated their expertise. Two truly great bomber pilots, Capt Ben Silly and Capt Duncan (Jock) Mackay, DFC, were commanding them and when a rash Albatros made head-on for Silly those behind saw his nose flick up and down. Scored by Vickers bullets the Hun shot over the next Four, looped wildly, and missed wing-tips by feet as it floundered sideways through the entire formation to its doom in a wood.

A second scout went on fire and split open from the tracers of 2nd Lieut C. W. Clutson. Relays of 10 and then 15 scouts sustained the barrage until Azelot was on the horizon. Unbelievably, after nearly six hours in the air, the squadron had come through with the loss of observer 2nd Lieut E. R. Stewart, DFC.

Their pursuit inside the Allied lines introduced a new combat element, which proved more effective against 104 Sqn as they returned from Thionville next morning. Three Nines failed to make base and were credited to *Jasta* pilots *Oblt* H-H von Boddein and *Leuts* Rudolf Klimke and Angewitter in exchange for two fighters.

About the same hour the DH 4s had strafed Bühl aerodrome, and when Fokker D7 No. 4461, totally covered by bilious pink, yellow, and green lozenge fabric, sneaked on to their tails as they sank to land the vigilant observers smartly dropped him in flames.

Mountains of cloud beyond Strasbourg prevented '55' continuing to Cologne on August 14 and Offenburg houses caught the cargo before the *Kests* closed in for a running fight. Setting down a damaged aircraft at La Matacuelle on the border-line Lieut Dunn was startled to find a Fokker keeping pace. The moment the bomber stopped rolling the German, imagining he was within home territory, made haste to claim his prize. Misjudging his speed also, he ploughed into a hefty hedge and stove in his ribs. A French patrol lifted him from the cockpit.

Generally this stalking tactic was less amusing to pilots tied for hours to a potential incinerator, chilled and listless from rarefied air and petrol fumes, nauseated by the stench of oil, leaden-muscled after juggling with a ton of aeroplane; or for observers, cold beyond thought from the slipstream playing on their backs, trembling with reaction after challenging death after death around the Scarff ring. 'The Lines' was a magic demarcation, outward-bound redolent of apprehension, inward-bound of safety. The disappearance of their psychological crutch was demoralising.

Ensconced in the verdant peace of London's artistic colony of Hampstead analysts of the Central RAF Hospital already were learning much about the abnormal burdens imposed by the newest warfare. Their studies of 200 'broken down' officers would establish that 167 were predisposed by heredity to nervous instability, a proportion little removed from that of Bomber Command a quarter-century later.

They would also discover that long-range and high-altitude operations had introduced extra stress factors. Observers caused special concern to Dr O. H. Gotch:

'It is generally admitted that an observer has a far greater strain imposed on him than a pilot . . . Any loss of confidence in his pilot will mean a correspondingly greater degree of anxiety in that observer.

'A crash—especially if the machine is falling from some height —will give him sufficient time to anticipate the fall in his imagination (whilst the pilot has his attention occupied in handling his machine) . . .

'Observers generally break down sooner and to a much greater degree than pilots . . .'

Typical of these patients was the 28-year-old Canadian whose de Havilland took a direct flak hit at 19,000 ft, fell uncontrolled to 5000 ft, caught itself, and then dived gently into the ground where it became a mass of flames. The Canuck, who had been alternately pinned by centrifugal force and flung around the cockpit for several minutes, was hurled from the aeroplane and physically survived with nothing worse than bruises.

Soon afterwards he complained of insomnia, exhaustion, and continual apprehension when airborne. He was watched for three days, at the end of which, after a series of nightmares, he collapsed completely and was posted home. The Hampstead specialists found him restless, ill-at-ease, with tongue, lips, and finger tremor. After a 'relaxation' course of bromide and long walks on the Heath he recovered sufficiently to undertake 'limited flying'.

But this officer had completed 100 hours on operations, and that was the minimum figure which offered the best prognosis. An aviator who broke down early in his career seldom flew again.

Dr H. Graeme Anderson listed six groups, which formed the basis for assessment of psychological cripples in World War II:

Stale—physically and mentally tired; Neurasthenia—predisposed; Toxic Element—history of illness such as oral sepsis, 'flu, or dysentery; Psycho—congenital liars, unreliable, obstreperous, supernaturally brave (a few 'aces' were in this category); Physical —lack of oxygen, air sickness . . . and Gotch found only one true case of oxygen deprivation; Malingerers—the bulk of those tagged 'Lack of Moral Fibre' in the later conflict.

The second and third classes, Anderson concluded, were often inextricable and although nobody had coined the term 'psychosomatic' these, together with most of Gotch's fear-induced anoxia cases, were of that nature. Only physical failures were curable and the doctors agreed that none of the rest should be returned to active duty. The danger of their spreading infection among sorely tried comrades was too great.

Meanwhile, an order forbidding COs to pass over those Lines had been rescinded; so on August 15 Major Pattinson led 14 machines of a revived 99 Sqn. Broken undercarriages and near collision in practice had not endeared the replacements to Pattinson and now their inability to nurse their cranky engines caused them to straggle across the blue. Worse, they failed to support 104 Sqn in the van. Three kept up, and these Pattinson took above Boulay aerodrome where fighters and ground machine guns punched holes in all the easily picked-out targets. To complete a sorry spectacle a laggard stalled at 200 ft on the Azelot perimeter, seriously injuring the occupants. But Trenchard, alert at this stage to the salve of encouragement, praised Pattinson for his refusal to abort.

Keeping the *Luftstreitkräfte* conscious of its own wounds became the main purpose of 100 Sqn, whose worth had grown apace since April 1917 when it had been the first official night bombing unit and twice bearded Richthofen's incomparable *Jasta* 11 in its Douai stronghold.

Clock hands moved to August 16, and the FE 2bs banked off the arc of Boulay, Friesdorf, and Bühl airfields which they had dented with nine 112-pounders and 74 Coopers.

After a few minutes Capt H. B. Wilson of Surrey glimpsed the wink of exhausts close together and gestured his pilot, Lieut F. R. Johnson of Oxford, to trail a mysterious aircraft sagging methodically.

HP or Gotha? Patches of cloud scudded away, exposing a line of unsteady lights 200 ft below and stretching into the distance. There was no doubt now, and Wilson's Lewis chattered through half a drum, red tracers zipping into the dark mass ahead. The exhaust flames tilted, and in seconds a black gap appeared in the lights underneath. The Fee banked sharply and had not completed its circle before a rash searchlight officer illuminated the ground, to give the excited crew evidence that the Hun had bashed itself into a tangle of wreckage across the flarepath.

In due course Wilson sewed the white-and-blue-striped ribbon of the DFC beneath his silver wings.

Came morning, and with it the bombs of '55'—barred by cloud from both Cologne and Mannheim—squiggling into the railway junction and engineering centre of Darmstadt. The *Kests* had been misled by the squadron's weaving and so delayed making contact, but the eventual battle was long and bitter, costing each side three aircraft. That, however, was no consolation to the capital of Hesse Republic.

Four citizens had been killed, four wounded; but a front-line aviator on leave observed surprise and fear to be intense. It was several hours before trains or tramways could resume service. Although Darmstadt had been a target-of-opportunity and was not touched again it lay in the bomber lane leading to Frankfurt, Mainz, and, on occasion, Coblenz so a housewife's letter is a fair indication of the disturbance any IF intruder could promote. She wrote: 'Many people are homeless and have no more dresses to put on. For several nights we have been obliged to get out of our beds. We don't go into the cellar, because with these machines you can be caught anywhere. When will all this be finished?'

Exactly a month after the bombing the *Hessinger Volksfreund* was furious with the authorities' paralysis. Public air raid shelters were not opened in time and factory workers were unprotected. 'To talk of remaining quietly at work is nonsense as we know from the last raid', commented its leader writer. 'When we remember that most of the factory floors do not even provide safety against splinters from artillery fire one cannot understand the lack of action in this matter.

'In all other towns in the air raid zone as soon as the alarm is given the workers have to cease work and take shelter.'

Elsewhere people had some right to complain. At Burbach, for example, where bombs were made the excuse for looting, professional criminals had established a particularly profitable black market in provisions, cloth, and linen. Everywhere during August captured letters sobbed the misery to Allied Intelligence . . . 'Nearly every night I spend two hours in the cellars' (Cologne); 'It is horrible, one has no rest day or night' (Metz); 'Yesterday the airmen were here again. I am quite ill with worry. You cannot imagine how scared the people are of aircraft, and my idea is to move to Bremer (a country town) where I hope the air raiders will give us a rest' (Coblenz).

The last thought was shared by many prosperous folk. Mannheim manufacturers, especially, moved to the university city of Heidelburg—perhaps persuaded by its great tun holding 47,000 gallons of wine. They, together with those who fled to other 'quiet spots' in the Neckar valley, were still within range but the woodlands gave an illusion of peace. It is doubtful if they cared but, their money apart, they were not welcomed by the locals.

'It is not the working man who thus seeks to bring himself to safety', said the sour and mutinous *Bremer Burger Zeitung*. 'Only those circles do this from which such as the "Fatherland Party" and the "Annexationist" gasbags are recruited, who can never have enough of this glorious war but who do not hesitate to run away with their precious heroism and cash boxes to safety from the enemy bombs.'

So long as there existed men with the determination and ability of Lawrence Pattinson, undaunted by distance or weather, the IF could make security anywhere in SW Germany a state devoutly to be wished—but not found. Shamed and depressed by the mound of bent aeroplanes which in two days his ham-fisted pilots had strewn around Azelot, at 1.40 pm on August 20 the Major invited the stalwart Lieut Walker to climb aboard and rose into ten-tenths cloud just above the trees.

Nobody but pilots who have flown by the 'seat of the pants' can really comprehend the amount of nerve required to envelop one-self in moist cotton wool with no more directional aid than a standard 5/17 Creagh-Osborne compass. Pattinson did this among switchback hills, deliberately setting course for Dillingen when at 5000 ft above, as he calculated, Pont à Mousson. Forty miles later he let down until the clouds parted sufficiently for a quick sight of his objective. He unclasped two 112 lb bombs with delayed fuses, and as the DH 9 reared away from a string of *flak* bursts Walker—whose confidence in his pilot was surely without equal—observed beyond the tailplane a flash from a blast furnace. The other bomb had struck a factory railway line. Forty-five minutes later Pattinson again came out of cloud, 10 miles west of Azelot but by exceedingly good fortune over flat ground. Trenchard had said 'bomb through cloud', and this intrepid pair had further proved that an entire mission could be flown in continuous overcast. But, predictably, the IF record they had established stayed theirs.

Any town could be caught napping by Pattinson's solo tactic. Even 12 machines could be elusive. Massed squadrons cut down their chances of escaping detection; yet they were the only convincing answer to the disquieting damage reports reaching Trenchard. For various reasons, sometimes in combination, aiming was ragged and such research as there had been indicated that the performance of the bombs themselves was little better. Provided it had been padded with sandbags or packed earth a small building withstood the blast of a 112-pounder which grounded six feet away, and of a 230-pounder within 15 ft.

The lifting power of day machines not extending to larger missiles the alternative had to be the biggest possible salvoes dropped in unison.

Extra aeroplanes should have meant extra protection had all the gunners co-ordinated their fire. That was not the case with 104 and 99 Squadrons as they cracked the dawn of the 22nd with their Pumas on the way to Mannheim. The climb to 12,000 ft exhausted a quarter of the leading flights' fuel, and there they discerned Quinnell's two flights widely separated and green Verys signalling the retirement of seven crippled machines.

Hagenau came up to port. So did 25 of its scouts, pulling hard towards the north. Abandoning hope of struggling another 60 miles Stevenson took the remnants of 99 Sqn to bomb the sparsely guarded aerodrome.

The Huns closed with 104, peeling off from 14,000 ft in waves on to the hindquarters of the Nines and there hovering just beyond the reach of the Lewises. The inexperienced crews blazed away, wasting ammunition, and straining engines with rough throttling. On the outskirts of Karlsruhe the EA made a series of quick dives, ending in fusillades which tumbled three bombers. C Flight, its double-diamond pattern shivered, was now composed of the South African deputy leader, Lieut Searle, Lieuts Lynn D. Merrill of Chicago, and Horace P. Wells, a university student of Boulder, Colorado.

Mist was creeping over Mannheim so, as the *Kests* drew off from the anti-aircraft area, Karlsruhe received the bombs. No sooner had the raiders twisted clear of the town than the scouts swarmed. Five made passes at Wells but he stuck close to his leader's faltering Nine, trying to cover him, until Searle curled on to his back and spun in. In that moment flying wires either side of Wells were severed and more bullets came up between his legs and thudded into the seat cushion which fortunately was stuffed with sand.

Jet black smoke and steam shrouded the DH 9's cockpits from the shattered oil tank and radiator. Biting back the pain of a splintered leg bone the observer, Lieut John T. Redfield of Montclair, New Jersey, was about to squirt the Pyrene extinguisher when the fire died naturally. Wells gained some semblance of control at 6000 ft with his wing slanting past Baden-Oos, in 1910 the landing ground of the Zeppelin *Deutschland II*. The crackle of a Maxim made him twitch round, and he found a Hun shepherding them to a dead-stick touchdown.

Workers, spanners upraised, surged to the Nine from the salvage depot based on the disused aerodrome. Violence, however, was prevented by the presence of the *Kest* pilot who formally saluted Wells and in return accepted a filigree butterfly 'charm' which the American unpinned from his helmet. He then took the prisoners' personal cards, later to have them dropped with a 'quite safe' note to their squadron. He also helped to fasten a tourniquet on Redfield's thigh.

The depot commandant was equally pleasant, but Wells had been warned that if forced down bombing pilots were likely to be killed and was afraid the water he was offered had been poisoned.

The Germans' procedure for IF flyers, by this time routine yet gallingly fresh for every recipient, was put in train—*Korrekt* farewells of 'for you the war is over', a swift journey to the nearest gaol (in this case, Rastatt), the calculated display of clever Intelligence—at Karlsruhe—and the end of the pantomime in Landshut *Kriegsgefangenenlager*.

For Wells there was a variation, soon to become the custom. As he was marched through the town the mothers of the Fatherland shouted, spat, and clawed at him; a display of gentle womanhood not unknown by Gotha pilots brought down in Britain. The difference here was that the burly armed guards made no effort to stop the hate.

So many scouts had peppered each de Havilland in the affray that only two *Kest* pilots, *Leut* Hinneburg and *Vfw* Prime, were given individual credit. All knew that this was a notable success, seven of the invaders failing to escape.

Major Quinnell became the second IF commander to scratch his broken squadron from the Order of Battle. Mercifully neither he nor Trenchard could know that he would do this twice more before the final victory.

# 7

*'And when they went I heard the noise of their wings, like the noise of great waters, as the voice of the Almighty...'*
*(Ezekiel 1:24)*

To the lay eye the IF's patched machines and sunken-cheeked personnel presaged the imminent collapse of the day offensive. Rightly inspired, however, men can endure until the body denies the will, and the professional onlooker merely doubted the validity of the exercise. For with the wasting of 104 Sqn and the equivocal revival of '99' Trenchard was to rely on the sorely tried DH 4s.

Somehow 'Alec' Gray would foster his men's morale, but could he preserve them physically? Strange accidents happened to knowledgeable and careful pilots, like Capt Taylor of '99', who without warning spiralled his observer, Bell, into the ground from 2000 ft. Their deaths were attributed to Taylor collapsing from nervous exhaustion. Sergeants led depleted flights, and observers were so scarce that squadrons borrowed from each other to make up the complement for a small mission.

Every week photographers found fresh landing strips where the interceptors refuelled to sustain their withering relay system of attack. Standing patrols formed permanent barriers along the arcs of Trier-Ludwigshaven, Thionville-Saarbrücken-Karlsruhe, and Troisdorf-Bonn-Siegburg, and they were also stationed in the environs of Coblenz, Mainz, Darmstadt (some cries were answered!), and Frankfurt.

Structural failure was less of a menace than in the RFC's time, but a London police-court case recalled it to the minds of fatigued pilots if vacant chairs in every IF Mess did not. William Smith of Tottenham and James Harding of Enfield were summoned for committing 'certain acts likely to endanger any person using an aeroplane'. After damaging a Handley Page spar they had filled a quarter-inch gap with soft waste, dangerously weakening the whole structure. That cost them each £10 4s—six shillings less than the basic weekly pay of an HP crew. But at least *their* wicked folly had been detected.

Other slackers, Government parasites and opportunist strikers, nagged perpetually at Trenchard's conscience. These were the men guilty of short-changing his youngsters. They should, but never would, pay for the supply gaps he espied during a tour of the squadrons:

'(55) No radiator and no cowlings. Gledhill bomb gear is incomplete. Ashes needed in front of sheds. AA unit under strength.
(104) Wants 20 Sidcot suits. Also short of brackets for baby bombs.
(99) Needs Armament Officer.
(215) Needs jack for 1600 lb bombs. Also an observer and gun layer.
(97) Not received Aerodrome Officer. Petrol system on O/400s was cutting out. Six big cowls don't fit. Want well-trained observers.'

The last two items referred to additional heavy bomber units under Major J. Fleming Jones and Major V. A. Albrecht, assigned to the 83rd Wing and positioned at Xaffévillers, east of Ochey and 15 miles from the lines. They, like the re-equipped 100 Sqn, and 216 Sqn, were possessors of Handley Page O/400s, essentially 1/100s with petrol tanks transferred from the engine nacelles to above the bomb cells. Much to mechanics' relief engines could be turned over by bottles of compressed air or by manual handle.

Several crews of 215 Sqn knew the look of *flak*. They had descried it on April 11 when they had flown out of Coudequerke near Dunkirk to co-operate with the Royal Navy in the initial failure to block Ostende and Zeebrugge harbours. One machine had been plagued by it for two hours as it prowled above the Zeebrugge Mole; and others bore the patched marks of hits scored during a brief round of raiding German back areas in France.

No. 97 was a virgin IF unit, but one which had enjoyed a unique glimpse into the future. At Netheravon it had begun train-in D/F (directional wireless), a form of position-finding enabling a navigator of strategic bombers to receive 'fixes' from ground stations—a system which, denied the impetus of war, remained imperfect in the late thirties.

As with other squadrons from now on, its flying strength would be composed of or replenished from innumerable RAF schools, spread it seemed on every cabbage patch in Britain and teeming with 18-year-olds whose rosy cherubic faces contrasted sadly with the sallow, seamed, masks of the 19-year-olds who had been in France before the turning of the Teutonic tide.

The cup of Mars was overflowing with rich blood from the British Empire, the United States, and—such is the miracle of regeneration—from the ancient island, whose Class of Spring '18 had not needed to be sacrificed immediately. In this year of the Deluge hundreds would not wear wings in time to beat the Armistice. Teachers, not eager learners, were at a premium.

The best instructors were a distinct breed, pilots whose professional skill was equalled by their aerodynamic and engineering knowledge, patience, sympathetic candour, and the indefinable ability to instil confidence. If fire in the belly, split-second reflexes, and superlative sight made 'aces' the instructors' devotion to the art and science of airmanship made them kings. Many would die, with the lunatic-strong clasp of a petrified pupil 'frozen' on the stick, to prove it. But this select company was thinly spread among 1600 pilotage instructors grooming and weeding the 22,000 influx of pupil pilots that final summer.

With no Somme or Bloody April or Hun breakthrough to counter, the schools took longer to prepare their students for service, added to which was the complexity of modern aeroplanes and the snowballing of ancillary subjects.

The average aspirant could expect his elementary training at a cadet unit to last 10 weeks before he was found a place at flying school. There he would sign for the Government issue of cap (helmet), gauntlets, Triplex glasses, leather jacket, thigh boots, Sidcot, overshoes, flash lamp, and—efficiency not kindness was the motive—a vacuum flask. After that he would be made or, as someone was any fine day on any aerodrome, broken.

Cadet Cyril Box, a managerial apprentice in the Bradford wool trade, just 18 and destined for IF night bombers, was such a one. He had been one of two candidates out of 39 to pass the RAF's recruiting committee, and it would take him a year to reach his Service squadron—which had not even been mustered when he offered his youth to the nation. But the immediate goal was Flying Standard Y.

Within days his best friend was killed in a Maurice Farman Shorthorn 'pusher', a 1914 relic, while on a routine exercise of 'circuits and bumps'. There were others, too, stalling, side-slipping, colliding. And others—'returned to regiment' or quickly posted away to office jobs. These were the skeletons cadets did not discuss. Loss-of-nerve was the unthinkable ogre at everybody's shoulder.

Box, however, made his four landings in neighbouring fields with engine off, flew in cloud under the alert gaze of an edgy instructor, and passed on to his 'speciality', bombing.

At stations with insufficient ground for a bombing range cadets had to make do with simulated bomb-aiming in camera obscura or Batchelor Mirror. But the majority dropped eight bombs from 1000 ft—'the four best must have an average error of not more than 40 yards from the target'—with the standard CFS 4B or CFS 7 day sight, and eight from 6000 ft using the High Altitude Drift Sight, managing to keep four within 200 yards of the mark.

After six weeks Box's record card certified that he was able to:

'1. Fly accurately and land consistently well at slow speeds, tail down.

'2. (Make) Three sustained turns, with and without engine, bank over 45 degrees.

'3. (Perform) Short figures-of-eight, climbing turns.

'4. Stall machine with or without engine.

'5. Sideslip and land off sideslip.

'6. Spin, half roll, and loop.

'7. (Be) Confident in clouds and rough weather and understand the theory of landing across wind.'

Passed on, he and similarly relieved cadets embarked on cross-country flights up to 60 miles, map reading, and pinpointing objectives on a route 'not defined by railways, rivers, or canals', and twice forced-landing outside the aerodrome. They flew 50-minute triangular courses and submitted two reconnaissance reports.

They also fired up to 100 rounds from a Lewis, changed four drums in the air, attacked an aeroplane silhouette on the tarmac with 12 shots, and real machines with the Hythe camera gun.

But, while the walls shook with revving engines and the summer breezes carried the ecstatic chorus of pupils on the flying roster, much of the time they were in the classroom.

More days would be spent in the hangars, fusing and defusing bombs and attaching them to racks; or in the wireless room, trying to send Morse at a readable rate of eight words a minute for three minutes, and to translate the spluttering key of an equally halting cadet. There was also a fearful darkroom, in which correction for wind, air speed, height, and level were applied on the High Altitude Drift Sight 'without light in four seconds'.

After such a mental stew the most ham-fisted pupil was thankful to make his night air tests, which consisted of six landings on a 'leading up' (intermediate) trainer and six on a Service type, a 30-mile cross-country flight, and a reconnaissance. On each category of aircraft eight bombs were dropped from 2000 ft with a CFS low-altitude sight and (not twice but many times more difficult to achieve than on the daytime test) the four best dare not be more than 40 yds from the target.

Accidents at this stage stemmed more often from over-keenness than inexperienced handling of the heavy machines; but Box was nearly the victim of two bizarre mishaps.

Up on an FE 2b he was making an approach circuit of the aerodrome belonging to the No. 1 School of Navigation and Bomb Dropping at Stonehenge, near Salisbury, at 4.45 am, with his observer, 2nd Lieut Lake (later with 100 Sqn), standing by to fire the warning Very signal. Came the moment, and as Lake squeezed the trigger of the stubby wide-mouthed pistol a gust of wind pushed his arm and the flaring rocket fell into the cockpit.

Whipping off his gauntlets he beat the flames into a reeking puff of smoke. Simultaneously Box snapped off the petrol.

The Beardmore died, but the smoke blew away and the pilot stretched a weak hand towards the gravity cock to put some force behind the windmilling blades at his back. Then it dawned on him that the 'office' lights were out. As he turned off the tap so his hand had knocked the other switch; and he was not very familiar with the Fee layout.

Height was running out rapidly and even as he groped Box saw they were in for a dead-stick landing in the dark, and in the field ahead whatever it contained. The Fee touched and ran smoothly; and not until they dropped over the side did they perceive that it had adopted the only collision-free route between a rash of grassy mounds.

Box's 'finals' at Stonehenge consisted of 11.20 hrs on the FE 2b by day, 5.30 hrs at night, 3.35 hrs on the HP by day and 5.35 hrs at night.

And with a total of 120 hrs airtime, 79.55 hrs of it solo, and 34.10 hrs of that in the type of night bomber he could expect to use in action—training that was out of the question 18 months earlier—he and his peers were classified as Long-Distance Bombing Pilots.

When they flew to Marquise Reception Park in France they had with them a certificate which read:

'He is a skilled pilot on his Service Type Machine, able to fly in all weathers and land correctly at slow speeds under all ordinary conditions, by day and night, with or without Holt Flares . . .' It added, a trifle cynically, '. . . is fit for Service Pilot as regards flying'.

Until the fresh intake could find its way around, the stress of very long raids was being borne by 216 Sqn, who detailed eight machines to tackle Cologne and Frankfurt on August 21, when they carried 550-pounders for the first time. One o/400 fell out with a misfiring engine. Then at 2000 ft over the French trenches No. 1466 almost came to a premature end because the searchlights 'challenged' belatedly and the end-on bulk of the departing machine prevented watchers from reading the reply.

A shell promptly exploded near the starboard wing, but, slightly subdued, the pilot, Lieut T. E. W. Browne, and his crew of Lieut J. C. Adams and Lieut Yelverton carried on; crossing shadowy woods and moon-silvered streams, edging past Zweibrücken, Kaiserslautern, and Alzey. They surprised an illuminated Frankfurt and at 4000 ft Adams moved into the front cockpit to con Browne on to the main station.

After a short run-in he tugged the bomb releases and the HP surged as the cargo whisked tail-down through the spring-loaded doors. *Flakgruppe* 6 went into action, making the sky a backdrop for their Brock's Benefit, stimulated by weapons imported since 55 Sqn's visit on the 12th, the total amounting to 77 heavy guns and six machine guns. Four searchlights had become 16, and Browne eluded one cone only by tipping his wings edge on to the beam. This desperate piece of airmanship baffled the operators long enough to dodge the angry sparks streaming up.

For 150 miles there was little interference with the ritual of food and song but when easing down towards Autreville, 216's temporary aerodrome behind the American base of Colombey-les-Belles, the port engine popped ominously.

Browne decided to make for familiar Ochey but the HP dropped remorselessly until with a mile to go the altimeter read 300 ft. Racing up was a steep valley, then 150 yards of open field terminating in dense woods. The temperature of the starboard engine was already soaring but Browne had no alternative. Applying full throttle he swung the machine into a wide circle to recover lost ground, meaning to place his wheels on the valley edge and trust the long grass to slow up the trundling juggernaut.

Then all power went. Stabbing the flare button he hauled the runaway into a caricature of a glide. He could not reduce the pace and the four wheels thumped at 70 mph—16 mph slower than maximum *flying* speed—and barely 50 yards from the dark mass of trees haloed by the white flare.

Browne yelled to Adams to get behind the seat and to save his own chest slid from under the control wheel, head cradled in his padded arms. The HP jumped a ditch and pitch-forked with the scrunch of a breaking box into a tangle of branches. Slowly the crew unfolded and Browne was solemnly putting his kit tidily together when Adams yelled a warning.

Coming to, the pilot realised the soft light had changed to a rosy glare and that flames were nibbling the starboard wing. He jumped 10 ft from the upturned nose into a bramble bush. From the rear cockpit Yelverton, still confused, calmly surveyed the leaping 200 ft fire. That is, until it reached the Lewis ammunition drums. With the first explosion he scrambled down to the others; but none could outrun the tracers which whined eerily in every direction. They fell flat, pinned down in the nearest depressions until the shooting ceased.

Trying though it was to be shot up by 'friends' twice in a night, daylight brought a further shock. Inspection of the HP's skeleton disclosed a shrapnel rent in the main petrol tank. For three hours the fuselage had been slowly saturated and they too cold to smell it. Lighting the flare had been tantamount to suicide.

The following night Lieut H. J. Miles and Lieut R. P. Kelly of 100 Sqn, flying a lone and penultimate sortie in an FE 2b, extracted the last ounce of destruction from one 112-pounder and eight Coopers at Saaralbe. Their salvo vanished into a chemical factory and two adjacent buildings, the old 'pusher' being tossed in the violent uprush of air. Altogether they blasted 100 chemical containers.

Had they pounced on a Fee in the air German pilots would have been assured of a satisfying conclusion, but '100' were so ungentlemanly that they preferred sitting ducks. In 48 hours they had blown up two machines landing at Morhange and Bühl and their latest nocturnal ramble took six of them to Volpersweiler, and the 19th *Armée Flugpark,* where there were 150 aircraft.

Aiming was good, and after a fire was lit it became better still. A second load fell across a wood supposed to camouflage the petrol dump, and the sky became so bright that it was remarked by people many miles away. A hundred feet of loading ramp was blown high against the flushed sky, and a 100 × 30 yard gap in this important replacement depot remained for a year after the Armistice.

At this bonfire the pushers were joined by 97 Sqn, who also bombed the railway at Ehrang and suffered their initial casualties—a third of the force engaged. One HP fell to 'flaming onions', the frightening but normally ineffective strings of green fireballs, rocketed in this case by Württemburg *Flamga* 925. Another carried its crew, including observer George E. Rochester, the novelist, to captivity.

A duo from 215 Sqn on August 25 approached the Badische works at Mannheim from the north-west. Pestered by AA and searchlights Capt W. B. Lawson glided from 5000 ft to 200 ft. He then had to restore power, the Rolls-Royce roar almost immediately causing a blackout. But in their anxiety to find him the *scheinenwerfern* swept down to the horizontal, giving him all the light he needed as he skimmed the factory chimneys. The bombs struck among buildings, although some had been dropped too low for the firing mechanism to work, and Lawson lingered to allow his crew to hose the area with Lewis fire.

Patiently awaiting his turn Lieut M. C. Purvis attacked from 500 ft; and the daring couple made their way home through thunderstorms. Twenty-two bombs had cost the factory £8250 in damage, and four more had blown off the roof of the dye works and stopped the freezing process for 12 days. The rest closed the Philipp Rheinhardt metal works.

Eight bombers in a backing-up group from 216 Sqn ran into turbulence which was overcome by just one, piloted by Capt Geoffrey Buck, MC, with Lieut Arthur R. Barter as observer.

Hail stung them for 45 minutes and pitted the fabric, yet they bombed from 500 ft and returned, long overdue and exhausted. Both were awarded the DFC, the citation remarking that they had undertaken 16 raids 'in a manner reflecting the greatest credit on them both'. A week later Buck was killed when he misjudged his landing angle and rammed the squadron's petrol store.

With such results Whitehall statisticians could work out the relative unimportance of day squadrons, six DH 4s and 12 men conveying the same weight of bombs as one HP and consuming 120 gallons of fuel against 54 gallons every 100 miles. Newall, however, had established the efficacy of round-the-clock operations. Thionville and Metz had been the victims of three consecutive onslaughts. Mannheim of two, in May; but high casualties and the contrary weather had prevented Trenchard from developing the scheme to any extent. Stuttgart received the treatment once in July; Thionville and Mannheim once, and Cologne twice in August.

The overcast stretched to 500 ft on August 29, but at noon the bark of Archie guns, muffled by Milky Way scarves of vapour swirling around the hillocks on which the batteries perched beyond Azelot village, startled mechanics applying cotton waste preparatory to lunch.

Running from the hangars they were brought up short by the petrifying vision of a Hun two-seater looming at them through the grey felt. As they threw themselves flat its undercarriage scraped the roofs and with an echoing burst of motor it settled down into a gentle but menacing circuit of the perimeter. The biplane tail and chunky body identified it as a Hannover CL 3a, deadly in both dogfight and strafe.

Risking the pilot suddenly breaking his ring o' roses several of the men pelted for the gunpit, clamped and swung a Lewis—seconds before the EA cocked up a wing and snarled into a high speed pass across the aerodrome.

Eighty rounds crackled, tracers inching towards the Hun, which rose sharply and turned away. Coughing from the cordite fumes hanging in the heavy air, the ground staff then noticed four Spad 13s slipping along the fringe. Simultaneously there came to them the popping of aerial combat. Unseen, a Spad crashed with its pilot dead from a bullet in the temple; but the Hannover, engine smashed, glided down 10 miles to the south.

The following Sunday it was exhibited in Nancy's Stanislaus

Square. The captive crew could not have been more disgusted with Fate and the weather. On 'ferry' duty they had merely been trying to locate Metz.

The salvo as a regular bombing practise evolved at this time, 12 bunched machines toggling in unison. The commander drew clear of his followers, steering into a suitable down-wind position and aligning his sights as the others closed behind him. As the target came up he shot off a white Very and everyone pulled the toggle.

Whenever the Met officers gave a favourable indication the General tried to start a run of bombing against one objective. By August 30, however, there had been such a spate of filthy weather that Cologne was almost recovered from the last gainful attack eight days previously. So 55 Sqn were assigned to halt repairs.

Amid the sky's grey muslin tendrils the two flights failed to unite, and battle-wise 'Jock' Mackay turned his team loose on Conflans 12 miles over. The other leader, new to this most exacting of posts, considered he should at worst try for the alternative of Coblenz. Therefore he waved his five companions on to Metz, and to their doom.

*Leut* Hellman's *flakbatterie* 573 scored with its first fusillade, Lieut William W. Tanney of Detroit feeling its concussion against the belly. Imperceptibly the machine sank into the unequivocal position of the straggler, cold meat for the zooming Frescaty and Metz flocks of *Jastas* 13, 65, 72, and the blue-and-white Fokker D 7s of *Leut* Raben's *Jasta* 74.

Four D 7s, two Fokker DR 1s, and two Pfalz D 3s jockeyed for a clear shot at the crippled bomber, two of them to starboard being sprayed by the observer, Lieut Gormley of Dublin. As Tanney recalled it: 'On the other side was a Fokker triplane, so close I could have hit him with a cricket ball. He had me and knew it. I knew it, too, so I ducked to the floor until I heard no more shooting and kept trying to catch up with the flight.'

Moments later two bullets ripped into Tanney's chest, one lodging under the right shoulder blade, the other striking a front rib and ricocheting to his diaphragm. They are still there.

His sight failing as his blood drained, realising that he was desperately, perhaps fatally, wounded, Tanney clung to the thought that he must fly a reciprocal course to save his observer. At 12,000 ft he went into a shallow dive, simultaneously peering for a landmark from which to take his bearings. Suddenly the right-hand instruments shattered, and another Hun was sitting on his tail.

Rapidly he flattened out the Four and made a respectable landing before passing out. The German taxied up and he and Gormley eased Tanney from his cockpit, around the back of which the observer counted 25 holes.

Meanwhile, Raben, *Leut* Wilhelm Frickart, and *Leut* von Bueren methodically chopped up the other de Havillands, in which seven officers were killed, although one riddled machine struggled home to a crash landing. With Tanney, Gormley, Papworth, and H. H. Doehler—another American—posted missing 55 Sqn's losses over 19 days amounted to 21 officers, plus two seriously wounded.

True, this butcher's bill represented more than half the full strength of a day squadron; but in military terms it was barely 'supportable'. In human terms it was far below any psychological safety margin within the experience of doctors.

Those officers—and they were not few in the IF, where perhaps 80 per cent of aircrew had not previously served Trenchard—who felt their commander remote and indifferent to them as people might concentrate on the relatively simple problem of personal survival. A really unfeeling world across the Channel ceaselessly impinged on the General, even his political sympathisers jarring him with their puerile philosophies.

Weir was as guilty as any; his latest notion being that incendiary bombs should be used on the slum areas of an unspecified German town where 'I would very much like [*sic*] if you could start up a really big fire . . .'

Theoretically, the reasoning was sound if not humane, as 26 years later the fire storms of Hamburg and Dresden, though freaks, would confirm. But none of the RAF's incendiaries generated sufficient heat nor could they be spread in quantity.

Warmed by this vision and disregarding the bombing principles underwritten by the Government, the Air Minister also urged: 'If I were you I would not be too exacting as regards accuracy in bombing railway stations in the middle of towns. The German is susceptible to bloodiness, and I would not mind a few accidents due to inaccuracy.'

Trenchard's dry humour was a personal safety valve. Remembering the *flak*, the fighters, and the crosswinds he replied sardonically: 'I do not think you need be anxious . . . All the pilots drop their eggs well into the middle of the town generally.'

His expectation of greater precision was not high, although the arrival of two virgin machines promised the IF a fresh lease. The DH 10 Amiens, a three-seater, could carry 900 lb of bombs for four hours, and was being tested by 104 Sqn. The DH 9A, a conventional two-seater resembling the Four but with the cockpits placed together, was with 99 Sqn who had found it heavier to handle than their own aeroplanes but otherwise superior. Laden with two 230-pounders it reached 15,000 ft in 47 minutes while the Nine, labouring under the weight of one, was 3000 ft lower.

Reliable transport was the minimum the IF deserved from the Homeland factories and the minimum required to replace 21 machines shot down, six lost to the elements, and 54 wrecked in the British lines after mechanical failure and pilot error.

By prodigious effort in assembly rehearsals irrespective of weather and in 'blooding' strafes on Bühl, Doncourt, and Morhange airfields '99' had transformed itself, and Pattinson did not hesitate to accompany 12 machines scraped together by 104 Sqn for a Ludwigshaven show on September 7.

At the preliminary conference he proposed a new ploy. Seventy-five per cent of bombers which dropped out did so above 10,000 ft, and to eliminate straggling and save fuel it was agreed that this time the four flights would ignore the rule of 'as high as possible'. In the event 99 Sqn took 40 minutes to form up and after a further 40 crossed the lines 1000 ft above and a mile in front of '104'. Gauging the situation accurately six Huns sneaked in, picked off the two rear men, and then forced down Pattinson's 'tail end Charlie'.

The Major slowed until '104' closed to 60 yards and, ignoring 15 EA circling at 11,000 ft, in that fashion they entered the town from the east. Down slid the bombs, nine hitting the Soda Fabrik; down slid the fighters, another '104' crew gyrating into the smoke. Eight Huns swooped on to Pattinson's right flank, and, with commendable confidence in his freshly trained officers, he executed a sharp turn towards them. Cohesion was maintained, and the blast of Vickers fire dissolved the Germans' resolution. They scattered across the sights of '104', and were last seen, tails up-wind up, low down on the horizon.

Pattinson, who added a DFC to his breast for 'skilful leadership and manœuvring', again had a worthy command. Quinnell was short of another five aircraft and the anguish he felt was echoed on behalf of Trenchard by Maurice Baring:

'Of all the experiences we had in connection with aviation I thought, personally, that there was nothing more trying, more harassing, and more hard to bear for those who were responsible than waiting for these long-distance raids to return . . . It was not merely a question of losing one or two machines. One knew only too well that a change of weather might occur when the machines were at a great distance and one might quite easily lose the whole formation.'

Once, the IF Staff were indeed in at the death. At 2 am on September 12 a US Army officer entered Trenchard's bedroom with the news that the St Mihiel Offensive had begun. Such was the Americans' security that Zero Hour had been unknown to the General, and this despite the agreement of full tactical co-operation under which his squadrons had been softening up lines of communication at Courcelles, Orny, Verny, Ars, and Arnaville for the past week.

Eight hours later he and Baring were on a hillock at Neufchâteau to see 39 heavy-burdened Breguets lurch through the rain into frowning cloud. One of the ungainly machines veered towards the party, its wing scraping the far side of the rise. Cartwheeling, it blossomed with flame, bowling the pilot into a still heap yards away. The observer fought free and tottered with smoke issuing from his heavy clothing.

Trenchard bounded to his side, sawing at the leather with a little gold penknife. While they awaited the ambulance the bombs went off. The General's biographer records that on reaching his car he found the driver trying to hide binoculars through which he had viewed the scene. 'Aviation is war, Chalcroft, not a sport,' he roared.

During the next few sorties IF crews had every right to complain that they had not joined to strafe masses in *feldgrau* tunics and coal-scuttle helmets—the first and last glimpse most would have of the German army—and fly photo missions up winding Moselle valleys while Maxims enfiladed them from *above*. Mechanics became sickened by the number of coughing de Havillands whose flat tyres sent them into ground loops, and by the bloody heaps in the exposed rear cockpits.

But, particularly for Colonel Mitchell's 'trainees', there was a rare satisfaction in this practical display of Anglo-American solidarity.

Within 48 hours the Americans' 400,000 men, 3000 cannon, and French tanks consolidated about two miles of territory, an advance so well planned and executed that already preparations for an Argonne push could begin. Vile weather handicapped air support and in fact the *Luftstreitkräfte* did not cause the IF concern until September 14.

That morning Capt W. G. Stevenson took six of 99 Sqn to Metz, a broken connecting rod and a misfiring cylinder depriving him of two within minutes of being airborne. Twenty EA attacked south of the town but everyone toggled. The bombs suspended traffic on the Peltre-Metz track for 15 hours, on the Metz-Peltre for three, and wrecked three locomotives in the shunting station.

Stevenson's gunner, Sgt J. Jones, drove down one scout and another limped away from the fire of Lieut H. A. Boniface. This prevented molestation of the newly arrived 2nd Lieuts G. A. Shipton and W. G. Ogilvie while they set down their crippled Nine.

Three against 18, and 47 miles to go. That was their sorry plight when 2nd Lieut James Gordon Dennis, who had been 15 days at Azelot, was slammed in the back by a bullet which broke up and perforated his intestines in a dozen places.

Weak and sick, he tried to signal his observer, Lieut H. G. Ramsay, with the customary elbow jab in the kidneys, and found him writhing from an ugly and disabling leg wound. Dennis realised his friend could not help him steer, and as lancing pain superseded his numbness and nausea the lure of Hunland a bare two miles underneath became magnetic.

His personal survival depended on quick medical treatment. But, the silk, wool, and leather layers of his flying kit glued with blood, Dennis held his station and effected a text-book touchdown on our side. Admitted to the 8th Canadian Stationary Hospital at Charmes, where numbers of the IF lie buried, his condition was labelled 'critical'. Four days later he was out of danger, such was the surgeons' quality and his own indomitable will.

And he was still in bed when General Sir Hugh Trenchard pinned the Distinguished Flying Cross to the sheet covering his breast.

This foray started the longest round-the-clock sequence ever achieved by the Force, eight raids in 192 hours during which every squadron concentrated primarily on Metz.

Immediately disturbing to the German Staff was the rate at which civilian morale was decaying. In six weeks the IF had increased its average range by 29 miles during the day, 21 at night, yet hitherto responsible civic leaders were screaming for peace. Not since the peace moves of 1916 had the Junkers been at war with the civil government, but with their armies near to exhaustion, immersed in the attempted repulse of the Americans, they were again being back-bitten by scared little men in frock-coats.

No less a personage than the gifted General Hermann von der Lieth-Thomsen, *Luftstreitkräfte* Chief of General Staff, made time to address the Town Council of Aachen.

'It has come to my knowledge that reports are being spread that air raids on a vast scale over Aachen are shortly to be expected,' he said. 'I hasten to state that there is not the slightest foundation for such a report.'

Very soothing; had he not then spoiled it . . .

'But as the geographical position of Aachen does not completely preclude the possibility of enemy air raids I beg that every possible means to obviate or mitigate the resultant dangers may be immediately taken . . . Only when the population is convinced of the importance of such protective measures, and takes adequate precautions, will there be any possibility of suffering no, or slight, damage.'

What the Junkers expected of the obstreperous civilians disfigured the walls of public buildings with Gothic print and brutal soldierly phrases:

'1. To be calm is the first duty of all. Panic entails greater dangers than does a raid.

'2. Seek cover in the nearest house. Get out of the street. Away from front doors and windows. Curiosity means death!

'3. Should the protection of houses not be available then throw yourself into ditches and recesses.

'4. At night time pay no attention to the attacks.

'5. Tie up horses.

'6. In the case of exploded and unexploded bombs a wide area all round to be at once evacuated and avoided, on account of the danger of explosion and poisoning. Touch nothing! At once send for the police.

'7. Avoid inhaling gases! Hold the breath and keep a damp cloth over mouth and nose.

'8. Telephone only to be used in case of fire, accidents, and dangerous illness. Connections are not guaranteed!

'9. At night time all lights showing to the outside must be screened.

'10. The spreading, without official consent, of news concerning air raids is forbidden.'

If this were tangible proof that the IF was exacting its own peculiar toll the evidence conveniently escaped the counsellors of Colonel Repington, *The Times* Military Correspondent and Field Marshal Haig's political sounding board.

For at this moment he attacked the policy that allowed aircraft to be withdrawn from the Western Front 'to bomb the apple women of Mannheim'. This despite his acknowledgement that under Trenchard ('brilliant, full of ideas, alert, combative, and a mine of information') the Force had prevented 200 German fighters from swelling the *Jastas* in northern France and Belgium.

By now Trenchard was able to brush off such partisan critics. But over the next few weeks his squadrons were to be vitiated by an insidious foe.

# 8 *'And again he sent another; and him they killed, and many others; beating some, and killing some.' (Mark 12:5)*

Since April medical officers had been dealing with a virulent type of influenza which had reached pandemic proportions but whose origin was disowned by both contestants. Whether it was the Germans' 'Flanders Fever' or the Allies' 'Spanish Flu' in the first month of its rampage it had put between 15 and 20 per cent of the armies in hospital, and the second wave now swept to the better-preserved regions of France.

By June there were a few easily recovered cases in the IF but as battle weariness set in the grip of the bug—not until 1933 classified as Virus A—tightened, until the late autumn saw deaths from its resultant heliotrope cyanosis which especially affected the young. In one September day 99 Sqn posted Lieuts Taylor, Beecroft, Walker, and American J. K. Speed, all veterans who had spent their last reserves of energy, to hospital. They had been dodging the Medical Officer for days. Those the virus missed were prone to nose and ear infections from prolonged spells at high altitude, chest and stomach disorders from fuel and exhaust fumes.

Oxygen, used by Zeppelin crews and on the Western Front for 12 months, was available, the supply being regulated by a control on the dashboard and gulped up an umbilical tube into a fur-trimmed leather mask. Usually it was switched on at 16,000 ft—6000 higher than in World War II—but the flow was erratic, the amount inadequate, the mask irritating to chapped faces, and the majority of crews rasped their lungs rather than clutter their 18 in square space.

Colonials, lungs developed by the pioneering life, were ideal high-flyers, hardly one of them failing to have the perfect capacity of 4000 cc. But, as air becomes one Fahrenheit degree colder for every 365 ft climbed and ground temperatures could be down to five degrees, they also were vulnerable to frostbite.

Zinc-oxide dressings and picric-acid solutions only slowly relieved faces and extremities transformed into fungoid horror by brawny swellings and sloughed black skin. Unusual merely in severity was the misery of the observer whose cheeks bulged until they were in line with the tips of his shoulders. It was a very strong heart that did not run wild from the pain.

It was mundane toothache, however, which deprived 2nd Lieut William Earle Johns of Coxhill, his regular observer, on September 16. As he and five other DH 4 crews approached Saverne, 60 miles from the goal of Mannheim, he had in the back seat 2nd Lieut A. E. Amey, a replacement so raw that his valise lay unrolled in the hut at Azelot. He was also jaded after the previous day's bout when nine out of 12 machines led by Capt Silly had surprised Stuttgart. Momentarily separated, Johns flew two miles ahead and aimed a 230-pounder at the magneto works before rejoining the formation. Most bombs strayed on to a housing estate, killing or seriously wounding 20 civilians. The retiring battle against 15 EA from Hagenau had been grim, although two Huns had paid in full for their persistence.

Now at 21,000 ft it was Johns' turn. Stinking black cauliflowers opened behind the machines, but a stray burst nearby, and the pilot was stung by petrol gushing from the riven tank.

With the altimeter abruptly wound down to 19,500 ft Amey recalled instructions and fired a green Very. Miraculously the curving light did not touch-off the drenched fuselage; but it did attract a pack of Fokker D 7s, believed to be early arrivals at Metz of Udet's *Jasta* 4, which had been stalking in the customary vulpine fashion and now cut off Johns' retreat. Seeking protection he pulled off his single bomb, opened the 'compensator'—which cut fuel feed and speed but also extended range—and clawed back to Silly's height. Strive as he might he could not reduce the interval and within five minutes seven or eight Fokkers surrounded him.

Manfully Amey triggered the twin Lewis guns, sending one Hun into a spin. But bullets snipped Johns' centre-section, cleared the instrument panel, and seared his right hip. Brushing glass from his splintered goggle frames he darted a glance rearwards, to see Amey crumpling below the Scarff ring.

Passing from a steep bank, Johns—formerly an instructor at No. 2 School of Air Fighting, Marske—stunted the heavy Four like a scout until he was down to about 8000 ft. When he pulled out a striped Fokker was clinging to his tail, and with that revelation came a Maxim burst through the new 375 hp RR Eagle VIII —probably the first engine of its type to fall on Germany. Power vanished, and Johns spent the next minute in tugging up the gashed nose. The machine's final swoop carried it straight for a peasant and his horse, who separated abruptly. Next in line was a clump of trees . . .

The impact thrust Johns' feet through the soles of his boots, and his 8 in. wide waist-belt tore loose to catapult his face on to the Vickers gun butt.

Bleeding from multiple wounds and lacerations he propped himself against the pock-marked fuselage, dimly aware that Amey was dead. He knew also that he was in Hunland. The punch administered by the first German *soldat* on the scene emphasised that.

Further rough handling was forestalled by his pursuer landing; and the battered *terrorflieger* was taken to Ettendorf village next door to Hagenau aerodrome. The physical ordeal was over.

Ahead, however, lay a form of torture unheard of since the imprisonment of Scholz and Wookey, the pamphleteers. With blood still seeping from his wounds, the pilot was transferred to the civil prison at Strasbourg and pushed into a room to contemplate Amey's body dumped on the floor. After a painful interval an officer, wearing a spiked *Pickelhaube* helmet and on his chest an Iron Cross, entered.

A *korrekt* man . . . Punctiliously he clicked the heels of his shiny field boots and saluted the dead observer. Then turning to Johns he snapped, 'So, you will be shot for throwing bombs.'

Remind himself though he might of an officer's 'rights' as a POW, Johns was more conscious of the borderline cases—the Nurse Cavells and the Capt Fryatts—in which the Germans had gone the limit. The 11 Sqn pamphleteers had barely escaped the firing squad.

The following days were long, dreary, and ulcer-breeding, with solitary confinement alternating with tribunals and a court martial. Periodically he was told that he would take the dawn walk, and he wondered why they bothered with a trial.

But Johns did not become an awful warning to the Independent Force. Maybe the war was too near its end for the Germans to take chances. Without hearing more about 'throwing bombs' he was unceremoniously packed off to a normal 'Kriegie' camp. And it said much for the unquenchable spirit of some men when he immediately tried to escape.

So far as the Force's HQ was concerned the most important raid of September 16 was the supporting one on Mannheim carried out by 110 Sqn, the latest addition to Trenchard's daylight strength. For this unit under Major H. R. Nicholl (later AV-M Sir Hazelton Nicholl, a relative of General Henderson), was fully equipped with the DH 9A, whose tests suggested it was the long-awaited miracle. Mobilised as an entity at Kenley (Surrey) the crews flew to France with the cowlings of their 9 Acks each bearing the white legend 'Presented by His Highness the Nizam of Hyderabad'—the world's richest man, so they said—and settled down in Lieut-Col W. D. Beatty's 88th Wing at Bettoncourt. The substantial living quarters had been camouflaged by Chinese coolies and were, according to one pilot, 2nd Lieut William ('Tim') Armstrong, the most conspicuous thing for miles.

The landing ground, too, was a disappointment, sloping against the prevailing wind. The turf, freshly ploughed and holed by field mice, became boggy after rain. More terrifying, the Bessonneaux canvas hangars had been misplaced and the pregnant machines scraped the roofs on take-off. In six weeks this combination of defects wrecked some 20 aircraft. And fitters had difficulty in learning the coil ignition system of the Liberty 12 which powered the 9 Acks.

The squadron was not rushed into action, two weeks being devoted to practice, followed by a strafe at Boulay when it released 2028 lb of bombs. Even so it was no fit consort for 55 Sqn on the Mannheim show. Its unsureness was too obvious in elementary routine. Two bombs shook off their shackles and bowled in the slipstreamed dust from two machines as they sped down the field.

Certainly the 11 who reached the town were unable to deal with the volume or quality of its defenders. His nerves worn out by trying to keep station at 17,000 ft and brush off the fighters one pilot dived low to bomb and was shot to bits. And into the vacant space popped an EA to finish his wingmate.

Mannheim officials were satisfied with their preparations, a total of 16 raiders having achieved no more than start a tobacco store fire which lasted until 6 pm, overturn two railway carriages, and damage 20 yards of track. The graduates of *Kest* schools at Warschau, Paderborn, and Grossenheim were exhibiting their value.

Lacking in battle wisdom 110 Sqn undoubtedly were, but not in courage. The cold was too much for one petrol pump which froze solid. Twin pumps, wind-operated by tiny wooden propellers, stood atop two 50-gallon tanks between the engine and the pilot—in this case 2nd Lieut Bradley, a civil engineer from India. Should the second fail the 9 Ack might never reach Bettoncourt. Gesticulating at his observer to fix his dual-control stick, Bradley dropped his safety harness and thrust a leg on to the wing root.

The slipstream punched him with 100 mph force but he bowed against the icy blast and prepared to lever himself alongside the thundering Liberty. As he balanced the machine veered and his feet slithered outwards along the trailing edge. Somehow he tumbled half into the cockpit, screaming to the gunner to line the nose with the horizon.

During a long minute Bradley braced himself for another attempt, and again stretched on to the fabric box rushing against the slate firmament three miles above a pitiless ground. Belly pressed to the engine he leaned over the corrugated Vickers barrel, wriggled his fingers through the centre-section wires, and chipped away the ice from the pump. By the time he had edged back to the controls all cylinders were beating rhythmically.

With 115 Sqn now ready at Roville, all the Handley Page units were represented among 24 machines which roamed that evening from Metz, Frescaty, Boulay, Trier, and Merzig to Frankfurt and Cologne. But they fared worse than the two-seaters. Enemy fire cost No. 215 four, '216' one, and the newcomers one. A fierce AA box barrage was reported at Cologne, where *Flakgruppe* 9 controlled a revised and formidable assembly of fireworks. One machine, hit by splinters, crashed at Dillingen and eight people were killed and 39 wounded when stupid sightseers withdrew the bombs from their cells.

Altogether the AA sent up 16,063 shells while co-operating with 173 searchlights; and their percentage of hits was greater than it had been 48 hours before when 40 Handley Pages made up the biggest strategic force Trenchard ever put into the air and three were lost.

But on the latest expedition visibility deteriorated from 'fair' to thick haze, and engine quirks forced back several HPs and caused 100 Sqn's only casualty.

The *Flieger Alarm* had functioned belatedly at Frankfurt, and when Lieut Johnson—victor over the Gotha on August 16—came into the suburbs they were suffused in a pale yellow glow. The observer, 2nd Lieut F. H. Chainey of Winnipeg, moved forward and still undisturbed by gunfire chose a path to the town's vitals.

Most HP observers used the High Altitude Drift Sight Mark 1A from the lip of the nose 'office', hunching over to adjust its jutting wire sculpture. Chainey preferred to mount the sight at the trapdoor in the rear of the compartment where he was less affected by wind and noise. So, after dropping the 'sticks' of four he had selected, he did not appreciate that one engine had stopped until he hoisted himself to check the bomb bay was empty.

Sprawled across the back of the co-pilot's seat he tried to shift the monster four-bladed propeller while Johnson alternately flicked switches and coaxed throttles, but to no avail. Within 10 miles their undercarriage was brushing the trees and they jarred into a ploughed field at Darmstadt.

Joined by Lieut R. C. Pitman of Saskatoon, who had watched their antics helplessly from the rear 'pit', they set the 0/400 ablaze and tramped miserably south towards the Swiss border. By dawn they had covered a further 10 miles and, their Sidcots slippery with dew, curled up in a wood to eat the emergency rations of bully beef, biscuits, and chocolates. At 10.30 pm they resumed the trek. Hours later, their paper-thin 'flying' soles and socks worn through, they went into a field of root crops. Though their scraped feet made it ludicrous to continue they gathered turnips and beans and, dodging a party of boys on a similar mission, reeled on. But a storm finished them. Drenched and dizzy they surrendered at a village police station.

They were transferred, foodless, to Mannheim and then, foodless, to an intensive interrogation by Karlsruhe's cunning Intelligence chief, *Hauptmann* Meier. They knew nothing, however, of the far worse pressures applied to Johns; but that was typical of the inconsistency in Germanic excesses.

While a full moon period meant thousands of German burghers constantly sleeping in their clothes the daytime flyers experienced everything from fog to wing-tearing wind and rain that at oxygen-altitude was the equivalent of ice needles. In the understatement of the age such weather was termed 'dud'. September 25 was clear, however, and the draught of 12 DH 9As fluttered hangars as they left for Frankfurt. Capt Waterous, DFC, the seasoned American with '55', had arrived in the RAF's new sky-blue uniform to drill '110' in the critical art of keeping closed up tightly. He had reinforced his advice with some doggerel:

> 'It's not the Pfalz or the Fokker scout,
> It's the Siemens Schuckert that we worry about.
> They do fly high—with the *beaucoup* speed,
> And we can thank our stars it's pilots they need.'

In the cockpits there was an additional precaution—walking sticks for poking ice, a consequence of Bradley's exploit. Still, nothing could save the 11 machines which reached the Rhine from 50 Huns who lanced from behind a molten sun. They huddled, almost overlapping their wings as Waterous instructed and criss-crossing their Lewis streams. But one de Havilland dived uncontrollably over the vertical before the target came into view—and that lay at the heart of a pulsating black ring formed by a 'standing' barrage of *flak*. The three curved roofs of Frankfurt station winked treacherously and on them 110 Sqn aligned its sights.

Sixteen bombs sidled down. They missed the railway by half a mile, some smashing workshops and lock gates, one blasting the Kaiserstrasse thoroughfare where a pedestrian died and seven others were injured. Reflecting the reasoning public's irritation with authority, the *Offenbacher Abendblatt* attacked the Wolff Agency for saying the squadron had singled out hospitals and churches. That, said the writer, was a lie 'ridiculous and malicious'.

In their turn Nicholl's men reported the ingenious pattern but inaccurate elevation of *Flakgruppe* 3. The four missing crews dismayed Trenchard far more; as did the news from Azelot on September 26.

Accompanying the dawn came the brain-mashing din of the Americans' artillery, a sound so intense that it sprang the petrol tanks of aeroplanes 3½ miles from the Front. This bombardment was the overture to the Meuse-Argonne Offensive, a confused and bloody struggle which would occupy General 'Black Jack' Pershing, the US C-in-C, for several weeks. Capt Welchman of 55 Sqn took command of No. 99, Pattinson having become CO of 41st Wing; and at short notice he headed seven machines to Thionville in support of the Push. Near Metz 30 EA engaged them, and in order to manœuvre the Nines dumped their bombs on the town.

Shot through the lungs Welchman landed his wounded observer, 2nd Lieut T. H. Swann, and lingered as a prisoner until repatriated to die at Charmes hospital after the Armistice. Lieut S. McKeever's machine was riddled and broke apart as he touched down, with fabric eddying like confetti behind him, at Pont à Mousson. Lieut H. D. West carried home his dead observer, 2nd Lieut J. W. Howard. Nobody else returned; and the squadron was left with three serviceable DH 9s.

Night raiders fared better. The new heavy bomb, the 550-pounder, was tried on Thionville junction by 100 Sqn; but conventional loads descended with greater violence on Metz. Six locomotives and a string of goods trucks and passenger coaches were hurled across the tracks where their mass interrupted traffic for 24 hours.

But at this juncture the Independent Force reached its lowest ebb. One day squadron grounded, the rest badly mauled; night squadrons frustrated by weather and fractious engines; and their role largely changed to one of tactical support.

Much as he desired to assist the American and French ground troops, much as he had always prosecuted the immediate war, Trenchard was afraid his thin branch of specialists would be whittled away. The Big Stick might not be there for the *coup de grâce*.

Commanders unclear about their objectives are in danger of achieving none, and there was an aviation precedent for Trenchard's anxiety. Plans made by *Hauptmann* Rudolf Kleine, commander of *Kagohl* I Gothas for large-scale attacks on military targets in Southern England had been rejected by German Army High Command which had confined him to moonlight raids interspersed with strafes on Haig's back areas. Londoners welcomed the relief and the extra suffering of the British Army was hardly discernible. Nor had the disintegration of a once proud and audacious group ended. The ultimate irony was now being enacted, the re-equipment of several *staffeln* as night fighters to engage RAF bombers hammering Gotha and Giant airfields in the north.

Hastening to London, Trenchard left Weir under no illusion that DH 9s could continue with their present power plant. Mechanical breakdowns alone prevented one in seven from reaching its target; and, recalling his nine-month-old prophecy that the machines themselves would be obsolete for strategic work by July, he said he could neither equate such crippling losses with operational necessity nor justify them.

There are former RAF officers who feel deeply that having been denied instant assurances of better equipment Trenchard should have resigned. Doubtless, *they* would have remembered such a gesture; but the wider world would never have permitted their benefactor to build the RAF which saved Britain in World War II; and among his contemporaries there was none with the unique combination of qualities he deployed in the vital Twenties.

The word 'deserter' haunted him from his spring resignation and in the event his absence could not have re-jigged the assembly lines and produced adequate aeroplanes faster. Or, as was indicated by 110 Sqn, transformed the eager school-leavers from RAF training establishments into war-hardened crews.

Besides, the primary reason for Trenchard's trip was outside the ken of junior officers—no less than the continued existence of the Independent Force.

In dogmatic memoranda during the month Marshal Foch had bid to net the British strategic bombers, and Trenchard—who was not unsympathetic to Foch's military aims—was constrained to inform Weir that the IF might well be abolished. The Frenchman would produce some courteous phrases but they would condemn the IF to his direction.

Foch's most aggressive assessment, on the 14th, had prompted this outburst. For he consigned the Independent Force to the main tactical body of Allied aviation, although it might 'in quiet periods, act on the morale of the enemy people or against enemy industrial establishments, which is its secondary function'. Any other course would be taken to the detriment of the armies. Therefore, at any given moment the role of the Force must be determined by the Commander-in-Chief alone.

For this Foch had the backing in principle of all the Allies' Military Representatives—Army Generals Belin, G. Sackville

West, di Robilant, and Tusker H. Bliss—on the Supreme War Council, who advocated an Inter-Allied Bombing Air Force, or Forces, 'exclusively subject to the General Commanding-in-Chief the Armies' in any theatre from which they flew.

At the request of Clemenceau, President of the War Council, Foch outlined his programme for 'the forces thus grouped (which) will be at my disposal'. And he reserved the right 'to use the whole or a part of these forces in battle, whether by dividing them among the armies or by fixing objectives for them in connection with operations either projected or in course of execution'.

Nevertheless, Foch had learned the lessons of 'distance assault'. The scheme, he asserted, demanded raids on a large scale, frequently repeated and methodically planned. Objectives had to be fairly easy to find, immovable, and sufficiently scattered to divide enemy defences and to allow for the vagaries of weather.

He enumerated the targets in order of urgency:

*Distant:* (*Chemical*) *Ludwigshaven-Oppau, Hoechst-Lever*kusen. (Industrial and commercial) Frankfurt, Mannheim, Mainz, Stuttgart, Coblenz, Friedrichshaven. (Shunting station) Aix-la-Chapelle (which meant Aachen—no matter what General von der Lieth-Thomsen told the town!)

*Near:* (Industrial and commercial) Karlsruhe, Freiburg, Saarbrücken, and railways connected to them. (Shunting stations) Ehrang, Karthaus, Offenburg, Remelfingen near Saaregemund, Saarbrücken, Hainsbergen near Strasbourg.

*Aerodromes:* To be attacked as the Bombing Air Force commander thought fit.

Secondary targets included the gunpowder works at Rottweil, the Mauser factory at Oberndorf, and Kaiserslautern. Missing from the list were vital objectives familiar to the Independent Force. The Lorraine-Luxembourg iron basin, which Foch acknowledged produced at least 75 per cent of Germany's ore supplies, was excised because henceforth it would be a responsibility of French Army squadrons as opportunity offered. So were metallurgic towns of the Ruhr and Rhine below Coblenz, 'owing to the distance from our lines and the present weakness of our resources in regard to the importance and number of objectives'.

Foch also accepted that the latter regions accounted for some 60 per cent of Germany's steel production but he was convinced that supplies could only be attacked effectively in transit—a stratagem to which Newall, with a ration of 46 aeroplanes, had resorted almost a year before.

The Marshal reiterated that only during periods of stabilisation after an offensive would attacks on the German interior become the new organisation's task. Moreover, he would not guarantee a fixed quota of machines for that purpose.

'On that basis' the Inter-Allied Air Force (at this stage the title was fluid) would comprise the British Independent Air Force, a French bomber group (Voisin 10 and Farman F.50 machines), an Italian bomber group (presumably Group VIII with the Caproni CA 3s of *Squadriglia* 3A, 14A, and 15A, which were already in France), and subsequent American flights.

Aerodromes were allocated in national zones, although the Italians came into the French sector. To facilitate some day operations fields outside the zones might be employed; but 'tenants' would be evacuated within 24 hours should Army squadrons require the space.

To the Independent Force this scheme was shattering, as it was slighting to the British and American Governments. It was stuffed with Gallic self-interest, narrow in its concept of future aeronautical development; yet in the context of the military situation at that period not unreasonable.

Germany was weakening but Foch could not date her collapse. He did, however, anticipate an acceleration of the northern (British) and south-eastern (Franco-American) offensives. As the drives progressed German industrial regions would become battlefields and bombing by Army Co-operation machines could then achieve tactical and strategical results. Accordingly the bulk of long-range work would fall to the really big-loaders, the multi-engined bombers in high concentration.

Historically, however, the bombshell was contained in the shortest clause headed 'Object':

'To carry the war into Germany by attacking her

industry (munition work)
commerce (economic crisis)
population (demoralisation)

'These bombing raids on the German population do not properly constitute reprisals—this like poison gas is a means of warfare which was first used by the enemy and which we are therefore forced to use in our turn.'

There it was, out in the open. Unrestricted area bombing, deliberately undertaken to kill, maim, and terrorise civilians.

To Foch they were all *les salles Boches*; and, standing on his blood-soaked native soil, he was untroubled by the civilised conventions to which the British would be paying lip service as late as 1944.

# 9 *'For the great day of his wrath is come; and who shall be able to stand?' (Revelation 6:17)*

Not only for Trenchard was the sun once more behind the Vosges. In October the IF was enveloped in chill fog and wing-shredding cumulo-nimbus, smothering worn-out engines, dampening human verve. Yet this was unmistakably the time when the Force attained maturity.

For the two-seaters there were no flights to industrial targets on 22 days, none for the night raiders on 16. They dropped only 98 tons compared with 179 tons in September, many Handleys being forced to return with their bombs tied up for safety as they tried to land in murk or with faltering motors.

But such was their grit and dedication that they spent 1828 hours (223 more) in the air. In the final fortnight 76 per cent reached some objective. Engine trouble prevented 14 per cent from bombing and the elements 10 per cent. Fifty-five per cent of those who toggled did so on primary or alternative targets, 20·5 per cent on those they chose in emergency. The 'missing' figure was 3·9 per cent.

Day and night forecasts seldom matched, but the round-the-clock endeavour was not abandoned, Metz receiving the bastinado four times and Longuyon once.

The hour was late . . . Since August 8, Ludendorff's 'Black Day' when the British Fourth and French First Armies had burst out in the Somme region, supported by 1900 aircraft against the *Luftstreitkräfte's* 365, the scent of victory had stolen across the battlefields. The initial successes of the Americans justified the health and confidence radiating from their sleek brown faces, stimulating their weary comrades farther north to a clinching manœuvre. In contrast the Fatherland everywhere apprehended the imminent defection of its dubious allies, and bitterly recognised the sunken frame of its own people. By October 1 it had surrendered 4000 guns, 25,000 machine guns, and 250,000 troops; by the 8th the Hindenburg Line which had obstructed Allied progress for almost two years had been overrun.

The Imperial German Air Force, hopelessly outnumbered on its Occupied fronts, short of petrol, spare parts, and almost devoid of tyres, continually regrouped to bring its maximum weight at vital points. Gone were the nibbling, defensive tactics and the urge for aggression was not far short of that in the Battle of Britain RAF.

Some of this excitement filtered through to the Independent Force, chiefly from the Yanks 'next door', but their war was as remote as the rumour.

Not for them the mad whirl above the smoking trenches, the homely washing lines of barrage balloons, the waves from khaki bands slogging past the aerodrome. Their war was the heart-stopping grab of a searchlight's translucent arm, the bomb's white puff hastily covered by swirling cloud, the change of an engine's beat above the forest, the cross-wind that shouldn't be there and consequently the landmark that shouldn't either, the five-hour juggle with height, speed, and distance to keep a wing tip from killing one's best friend; the endless, lonely, crawl through a dank, perhaps dark, tunnel of terrors.

That was 'Long Range' as the IF had come to endure it; and only beneath the sea could there be found a comparable way of death.

So their personal battle went on with the latest 0/400 draped across the perimeter hedge or a smouldering de Havilland being gulped by a cloud to denote the passage of another day, another show. A few of those days would be relived years later in sweaty nightmares. Like October 5 when turbulence and interceptors prevented 110 Sqn from reaching Cologne, Coblenz, or Ehrang, and destroyed four DH 9As and eight officers—a third of those who had tried. Unobserved bombs which burst on Kaiserslautern and Pirmasens were poor consolation.

Reports during the first fortnight refer continually to 'very bad visibility', equipment malfunction, and 'returned' aircraft, the only substantial success being on the night of the 9th when six HPs of 216 Sqn plastered Mézieres, Thionville, and Metz. Hardly a burst could be claimed but one bomb detonated the powder magazine on Metz Wiese island and the instantaneous blaze, which could not be quenched for four days, penetrated the beige haze wrapping the raiders.

Twelve days later 110 Sqn again undertook the long haul to Cologne. A conking engine let down Lieut Aitchison, deputising as C Flight leader for 'Tim' Armstrong, himself acting-commander, within sight of the aerodrome. The remaining 11 progressed 20 miles beyond the Lines before a squad of Huns interfered. Smart Lewis fire kept them to their cautious distance, but running into a range of piling and tumbling cumulus the 9 Acks' neat arrangement disintegrated. Groping among the cloud canyons north of Frankfurt they wandered in ones and twos down smoky alleys where they ran against the sharp noses of Albatros and Pfalz. One flared above Dillingberg; others smashed on the outskirts of Berenbach, Lauterbach, and Weiler. These were machines piloted by Lieuts King, and Sanders—of the denuded C Flight—Evans, Pearson, Reynolds, Wendover, and Mucklow. The survivors deposited their bullet-pocked hulks all over Meurthe-et-Moselle and Meuse.

There 110's major participation ended, and increased Trenchard's conviction that future squadrons from Home Establishment would need a leavening of pilots with war experience.

Sickening though this blow was the exploits of 100 and 97 Sqns at Kaiserslautern that night were a palliative. The newer unit released one 1650 lb SN bomb, about 20 ft long and slung in chains under the fuselage as no bay could accommodate it, and this hit the courtyard of the Greist munition works (pre-war, an American sewing machine factory) in Mozart Strasse

*Flak* sparks were swallowed in the refulgence of the explosion, the entire 100 square yards of the three-storeyed building being spewed from its foundations. Masses of rubble crashed on to a cellar where 50 people were sheltering. While rescue teams dragged out survivors 100 Sqn's solitary Handley Page arrived over the north-east corner of Kaiserslautern and sprinkled 14 cases of incendiary material, which started three fires. By their light the pilot aimed a 1600 lb SN (weights varied, up to 1660 lb) which buried itself in a field nearly 100 yards from an estate. Nevertheless, the blast smashed 15 houses and, according to a German report, 'the whole quarter was extensively damaged'.

Two nights later the three AA batteries placed on hills around Wiesbaden, partly to protect Mainz and Biebrich, aroused the

80,000 inhabitants of this restful watering place where the Kaiser had a residence and British tourists had once enjoyed the 30 hot springs.

The opacity was such that the town's night-capped worthies could not see the shell explosions and, undisturbed throughout the war, were enraged when the clamour continued for 30 minutes. Only then—and afterwards they alleged the firing attracted the invader—did they hear the drone of an o/400 from 97 Sqn whose pilot's brief read, optimistically, Mannheim chemical works, Essen Krupp works, Mézieres railways, Frankfurt factories with alternatives of Kaiserslautern and Saarbrücken. His indeed was a roving mission.

The 1650-pounder pierced No. 6, Riehlstrasse, pitching the roof and two walls into the street. Three adjoining houses were wrecked, roofs, doors, and window shutters being ripped from several others. Twelve people died and 36 were badly injured. Forty engineers led civilians in rescue work until the following afternoon and the fire brigade was 'damping down' for three days.

More SN bombs were rightfully directed on to the Burbach works, Saarbrücken railway station, Kaiserslautern, and Metz by 100, 215 and 216 Sqns, causing great havoc.

At last the IF had a really powerful weapon, and the promise of bigger and better things from the aerodynamic experts who had begun a stockpile of 1700- and 1800-pounders. The greatest secret, kept by a select group since Newall began operations 12 months previously, was in a shed at Bircham Newton in Norfolk —an aeroplane capable of raiding Berlin from England, 420 miles by the straightest route.

The Germans had built bigger, though not much bigger, bombers than the Handley Page V/1500 but none so portentous, and its masters always called it the 'Super Handley'. The length of its fabric-and-plywood-covered box girder structure was 64 ft, the height 23 ft, the span 126 ft, and the wing area 3000 ft. Equivalent figures for the o/400 were 62 ft 10 in., 22 ft, 100 ft, and 1648 sq. ft.

Without power plant its basic price was £12,500, more than double that of the o/400. Four 5 ft diameter wheels alone cost £540.

Its four 375 hp Rolls-Royce Eagle VIII engines, arranged in tandem under two cowlings, drove 13 ft 5 in. twin-blade screws at the front and 10 ft 4 in. four-bladers at the rear. They pulled and pushed it, and fuel for six hours' flight, at a top speed of 90·5 mph.

A big aeroplane, then, and also a revolutionary one, with the first practical tail gunner's Scarff turret between the four fins. A gangway connected the rear man with the mid-upper gunner.

Complementary to this marvel was the Grand Slam of 1918—a 3300 lb bomb, heaviest of the war.

The cat-eyed men entrusted with extracting the maximum from both arrived from Western Front FE 2b squadrons. They joined 166 Sqn of 86th Wing, which belonged to 27 Group, newly formed by a Canadian, Lieut-Colonel R. H. 'Red' Mulock, a former naval bombing pilot and Zeppelin strafer. There was another Wing, the 87th; and, in keeping with the mysteries of Bircham Newton, its ultimate destination of 'IF, France' was just a cover story.

Unfortunately, their fervour to start something fresh in air warfare was not duplicated among engineers, for the Super Handley had not been trouble free. Over the months defects had shown up in directional control response, longitudinal stability, and engine behaviour. On its 14th test flight one model had crashed and burned at Golders Green, the tail-gunner being the survivor from six occupants.

Modifications had improved overall handling but there were various opinions about the wisdom of installing the RR Eagle, the most powerful British engine in stock but merely an uprated version of a plant originally intended for comparatively light aeroplanes.

Deliveries of Libertys from the United States had ceased, however, and the alternative, a 500 hp Galloway produced by a Dumfries engineering firm, was unproved. Besides, all Handley Page fitters were well attuned to the Eagle; and in those days when maintenance was a cottage industry and improvisation an aerodrome art the readiness state of any bomber squadron depended on its brand of mechanics. A goodly share—so reported the Recruiting Centre at London Polytechnic—were B.Scs, and otherwise would probably have passed the Matriculation examination. They had to be dexterous and alert as well as mechanically knowledgeable. A 'remaining' engine could suddenly come to life and brain them with a kick of the propeller.

To turn over an Eagle on the V/1500 or 0/400 the mechanic

stood on the front spar of the bottom plane, hanging on to a cross-strut between engine and fuselage. From this uncomfortable stance he 'primed' the motor—and how much mixture to give was something between him and a special saint known only to good ground engineers. Muscle was then applied to the starting handle which turned the crankshaft to 'suck in', again 'just enough'. On the pilot's shout of 'contact!' the A/M switched the Ford coil and twirled the starter.

With luck the engine would bellow and the fitter drop on to the undercarriage, ducking from the whirling blades streaking his hair.

Under operational conditions that happened all too seldom, and the ritual would be repeated until the pilot—always the pilot—lost his temper.

The permutations of engine trouble were endless, from dirty spark plugs through snapped springs to loose jets in a throttle barrel—and on an Eagle-powered Super Handley there were 48 cylinders, 16 magnetos, and 16 carburettors.

So Mulock did not encourage outsiders in their desire for unfamiliar installations. He preferred ample numbers of the present product, and he still awaited those. Beyond that he required only Trenchard's instructions.

Despite tentative talks he had had in London about a new command the General had none to give. All depended on the reactions of Lloyd George, advised in good measure by Weir, to the Foch memoranda and the subsequent pressures of the Army-dominated group of the Supreme War Council. His plans, nonetheless, were immense.

How radical they were can be grasped when it is appreciated that only five years before pilots had copied the birds in all but wing movement. They flew a few miles from a nest and back to it. Now they flew longer distances and at night. But, except through misfortune, they came back to the spot they had started from. Any other procedure was incomprehensible, particularly to the tidy military mind.

Trenchard determined to create a truly mobile air arm—a shuttle service, with bases uniformly equipped to deal with several types of machine, their personnel trained in nonstop traffic control. Eventually the enemy would never know from which point of the compass the next assault would develop, or, until it was too late, the raiders' exact retirement course.

The scheme hinged on there being a group of aerodromes at a sharp angle to Nancy. Providentially, the Austro-Hungarian Empire was on the verge of disintegration and Trenchard had marked Prague in Bohemia, 300 miles north-east of the IF GHQ, as the third pivot.

Given his triangle, a Super Handley from Norfolk could fly to Berlin, reload at Prague, and bomb Essen, Düsseldorf, or Dortmund on his return journey. Even with de Havillands and 0/400s Munich, Salzburg, and Regensburg would be open to sorties from Prague. More devastating combinations would be possible with the Vickers F.B.27 Vimy, a three-seater bomber powered by two RR Eagle VIIIs and an endurance of 11 hours at a top speed of 98 mph. One had reached the IF for evaluation trials.

On October 26 the General finally received his new brief. Under an agreement reached between the British and French Governments and transmitted, through the Supreme War Council, to the American and Italian Governments 'for approval', he had become Commander-in-Chief of the Inter-Allied Independent Air Force (IAIAF)—a title suggestive of an Anglo-French diplomatic tussle for equal recognition.

It was virtually a carbon copy of Foch's recommendations to Clemenceau. The object remained 'to carry the war into Germany by attacking her industry, commerce, *and population*'. Raids were to be on a large scale, and to be carried out methodically, repeatedly, and with tenacity.

The restrictions also remained. 'Requirements of battle' were to be met first, although the Force's inevitably reduced strength in those circumstances was still to pursue its vigorous bombing.

Trenchard's staff would be augmented by representatives of all the contributory Powers. Operationally, he would answer only to Foch. Administratively, he was chained to France's Eastern Army Group.

However, his IAIAF shackles do not appear to have weighed heavily on Trenchard who was, after all, Army-bred and knew considerably more about soldiers than they did about aviators. Difficulties could be dealt with when they occurred. America's aircraft plants, now getting into top gear, could be relied on to provide enough machines. The 'shuttle service' would widen the Force's horizons sufficiently to remove it from Foch's immediate purview and two of its bases would scarcely interest the Eastern Armies.

Nothing could disguise a fundamental change of policy, the directive to bomb the Germans as people. A loophole was discernible, however, in the formal agreement, which lumped 'industry, commerce, and population' together, whereas Foch's memorandum had listed them as separate targets to accomplish specific aims.

Having matched squadron claims with Intelligence reports Trenchard well appreciated that bombs that failed to fulfil one task in the order invariably accomplished the other. When bombs were 'salvoed' in formation from 15,000 ft the average error was 3½ degrees, the equivalent of 308 yards, and when toggled individually 425 yards; that is, in a clear sky with all the fighters asleep and all the *flak* gunners at their sister's wedding.

So far the IF had not encountered such conditions, nor did they on October 28 when four Handley Pages of 97 Sqn were beaten by the weather, only one piloted by 19-year-old Lieut Peter Hopcroft of Cheltenham, for five months an instructor on 'heavies', feeling its way into Mannheim where it scored with a 1650-pounder. Experience could do only so much, and neither Hopcroft nor his crew survived the return trip.

Nine machines from 215 Sqn, aiming for Cologne, were caught in fog and heavy ground mist, eight being forced back and the other bombing Écouviez railways—which eight of '216' failed to reach, although six bombed Trier, Thionville, and Saarbrücken through layers of murk. Mannheim and Frankfurt defeated six '100' machines, one toggling on its own initiative into Longuyon. That town and Thionville also received the cargoes of three out of four o/400s despatched by 115 Sqn—whose motto became, appropriately, 'Despite the Elements'—for its ninth raid.

Thirty-three sent; 21 failed to bomb, one crashed, three officers died—all due to weather . . . Huddled in their moist Sidcots, eyes bloodshot and flooding from the cold and sulphurous air as they strained for a recognisable pin-point, the crews had striven their utmost to injure the Germans' *means* of waging war. With no idea what their bombs did but anticipating that they had killed some civilians, they could only pray they had weakened the Germans' *will* to wage war. At least Foch could not complain.

So hard had fitters and riggers toiled that altogether 28 o/400s were contributed by units next night. Two machines of '97' and six of '216' released over Mannheim, wrecking several shops of the chemical and aeroplane works and damaging the Lindendorf and Neckerau districts. According to the Germans the HPs' homeward trails to the south-east were unorthodox and resented by the nearby towns of Hockenheim and Durkheim which sampled the fruits of militarism for the first time. Heidelburg, too, was struck—and that ensured a disturbed sleep for the absentee landlords of Mannheim.

There were five deaths and 30 people injured, and further casualties were caused at Pirmasens, Offenburg, Thionville, and in the Burbach works at Saarbrücken. Static box fire was encountered in several regions, one '215' HP failing to return. None of the five sent by 115 Sqn completed the mission.

With the bleak dawn of October 30 all the *Kests* became *Jastas*, numbered 82 to 90, and eight of their pilots intended to celebrate the occasion when Capt Sanders led B Flight of 99 Sqn over Bühl aerodrome. The squadron were now expert aerodrome strafers, Frescaty and Morhange being favourite prey, a hangar at the latter having been demolished a few hours earlier when Capt Thom dropped three 112-pounders while testing a DH 9A.

This time a Nine turned back with a spluttering motor and a shell splinter broke another's propeller as they passed the Lines. Soon the Pfalz were dogging them and when Sanders sent off a white Very for simultaneous release of the 230 lb bombs they spurted forward.

Two concentrated on the deputy leader's machine, in which the observer, Lieut Wilfred J. Tremellen, was intending to load the camera. Tremellen had been with '99' barely a month, but he was well schooled in the Poor Bloody Observer's onerous responsibilities. Besides keeping a sharp lookout for the Hun above and below, firing Very signals, and feeding plates into the Williamson LB, he was the man any fighter had first to eliminate and therefore a standing Aunt Sally. Miserably cold even under a sun the strongest PBO never found the Lewis gun an easy weapon to keep in play aboard an aeroplane.

With a 100 mph slipstream beating the PBO's back and pushing at the barrel if it moved a few inches above the fuselage or outboard, with tracer bullets perhaps zipping from two or three directions, it needed extra fast reflexes and a stout heart for a Lewis handler not to forget duty and duck to the illusory protection of the floorboards.

Nor could the observer spatter bullets wildfire. In a minute the stripped airborne version of American Major Isaac Lewis's invention spat out 850 rounds, and the normal supply to de Havillands was seven drums holding 97 bullets apiece. To change a drum in the howling gale was a feat requiring strength, knack, and determination. More dangerous, though, were the stoppages of bulged rounds or slackened springs which resulted from long bursts and left gunners defenceless at a severe phase of a combat.

Add to these snags any IF observer's personal care of the whole flight by mingling his fire with that of the neighbouring machines and the ordeal Tremellen faced is barely comprehensible.

One Pfalz, with the unexpected armament of three synchronised Maxims, perched under the DH 9's tail but Tremellen, dismissing the holes magically punched along the fuselage, aimed at another Hun squirting his flank machine.

Cross-fire was not feasible with that number of aircraft and the observer's face was jerked forward by an icy stream of petrol spurting from the torn gravity tank in the centre section.

Blinded, his pilot made a sloppy left turn and the wing crashed into his right-hand partner. For a moment the Nines ground together. Then in a flutter of fabric Tremellen's 'bus wrenched free and, aileron askew, went into a fast sideslip.

A thousand feet under the others control was restored—but the Pfalz had not been shaken off. Once more came the flicking noise of slugs piercing linen. Desperate because only momentarily could he see the Hun, cunningly tucked into the 'blind spot', Tremellen depressed his twin Lewises and aimed at the rear of his fuselage! A quick burst coming through the skin from an impossible angle should shift any scout. Equally it could dislodge the tail unit; but Tremellen was at white heat.

He squeezed the triggers, the first bullets leaped into action—and the drums stopped whirring. For both to pack up at the same moment was beyond belief. But this was to be a flight of miracles.

The Nine was zigzagging frantically with Tremellen beating at the jammed guns when suddenly he discovered the Pfalz pilot was in similar plight and had turned aside, either out of ammunition or to clear his Maxims.

Seething, the tormented observer began to fire red, white, and green lights at the Hun as fast as he could reload the Very pistol.

Jibbing at the proximity of the fiery tentacles the Pfalz pilot zoomed, into the sights of 2nd Lieut G. M. Power, Sanders' gunner. Two seconds later he was plunging down, his exploded petrol tank pouring smoke through the tattered formation.

On the final turn into Azelot the damaged aileron collapsed and Tremellen's Nine, more of a sieve than an aeroplane, whacked down in a swirl of dust and flying woodwork. Tremellen slapped his pilot's shoulder. It had been his 13th show.

He had seen nothing of the IF's newest acquisition, a supporting scout unit which had moved to Bettoncourt as part of 88th Wing. This was 45 Sqn, commanded by Major A. M. Miller, DSO, which after a memorable career on the Western Front had spent nine months in Italy and destroyed 114 EA for the loss of six machines. Its renowned air fighters included Capt C. E. (Spike) Howell, DSO, MC, DFC, Capt R. J. Dawes, DFC, Lieut R. J. Brownell, MM, and Capt J. Cottle, DFC, who was credited by the British with shooting down *Hauptmann* Frank Linke-Crawford, commander of the Austro-Hungarian Flying Company 60 J and himself the victor in at least 27 combats.

But Trenchard decided it was wrongly equipped. He was looking for machines that could accompany the de Havillands wherever they might roam, and the endurance of No. 45's 130 hp Clerget-powered Sopwith Camels, superb in a dogfight, was two and a half hours. He forbade them their escort role until they received the Sopwith 7F 1a, a special version of the Sopwith Snipe which was replacing Camels in the north. This had been built to his requirements, an extra fuel tank shaped as the pilot's seat giving four and a half hours' flying time. In addition he anticipated the provision of Martinsyde F.4 Buzzards, adapted for long-range work.

Therefore 45 Sqn was confined to Line patrols, chiefly for the discouragement of strafing Hannovers and reconnaissance Rumplers which the Camels could reach, if stripped to bare essentials, at 24,000 feet. Hamstrung though they were the IF's only scouts brought down two Huns before Cease Fire.

Low clouds and rain again ensured on the last day of October that Foch's third objective was obeyed, 12 DH 4s setting out for the Deutz works at Cologne but undershooting by 15 miles and ravaging Beethoven's birthplace of Bonn, a truly 'undefended' university town. Through a hole in the freezing overcast the comparative brightness of railway lines attracted the leader. Fearing to lose more of his Fours with flooded carburettors—three had turned back through the intermittent rain with coughing engines, and another had become separated—if he pressed on, at 3.20 pm he pulled the toggle.

The salvo was swallowed, and in its drunken progress through the dirty grey layers crossed the railway. One bomb mashed 16 bystanders at a tram stop, another chose a crowd of innocent shoppers. Altogether 29 died and 57 were wounded. Pilots of the Fours which aborted actually completed a more useful military operation, dumping their loads on Trier tracks and Frescaty as they straggled home.

Only one Azelot bomber worked on November 2nd. Capt. Sanders flew his DH 9A to Avricourt junction, seven miles from the Lines. Sighting at 2000 ft after emerging from dense cloud he liberated three 112-pounders as he approached an ammunition dump. The shattering explosion was signalled by a fast-rising funnel of multi-coloured smoke.

No. 104, willing but incapable of tackling any substantial targets since October 23, valiantly put two full flights into nine-tenths overcast the next day but, unable to locate Bühl airfield, settled for the railways at Lorquin. A pilot was taken ill and two others also quit with dud motors. 55 Sqn abandoned its journey to Cologne and pasted the railways at Saarburg. November 4 was impossible, and when two 0/400s from 115 Sqn ventured aloft late the next evening bound for Morhange and Frescaty one lost power and bombed Dieuze.

Piffling though these efforts now appear they were wearing for the participants and required skills inconceivable earlier in the year. They also exemplified the IF's resolve to belabour the foe until his death gasp, which even these cut-off men assumed to be a matter of weeks and more probably days.

None among them felt less fulfilled than Trenchard. This should have been a triumphant week, with his highly efficient Wings ramming the German paunch, driving the Hohenzollerns and their Junkers to the conclusion that their Fatherland was morally and industrially bankrupt.

With the upsurge of the German Communists (Spartacists) or similar Socialist Fifth Column in Cologne, Kiel, Wilhelmshaven, Hamburg, Düsseldorf, and Oldenburg, and gaining varying degrees of support throughout the Rhineland, Württemberg, and Bavaria the door was unlatched. Perhaps ajar . . . to judge by the actions of General Lossberg, commander of the Army of Lorraine, who had established his own Soviet. The IF, for the

IAIAF was as yet merely a name, should be blasting it off its rusty hinges.

Ever since the Austro-Hungarian Empire's surrender on the 4th Trenchard had expected a summons from Foch's headquarters at Senlis. When it came he and the Marshal's aides swiftly drew up detailed plans for the 'shuttle service'. A French pilot would be in charge at Prague; and immediately the General arranged an expedition, including a train carrying a month's supplies for six 0/400s, to depart for that city.

He also sent the impatiently awaited signal to Lieut-Col Mulock in Norfolk. Three Super Handleys would be prepared for November 8. Target: Berlin.

Though GHQ operators had seldom been so busy they would not have changed seats with crewmen of 55 Sqn as, having unloaded over Saarbrücken's Burbach plant and Hattigny aerodrome, they were waylaid by 25 scouts. The EA fought ferociously, carving strips from the huddled Fours as they drew slowly away, hacking down four head-on opponents to clear an escape route. Lieut Richardson's machine dropped away, surrounded by a mass of snipers.

Spewing oil and petrol, trailing wires, their fuselages like colanders, the others landed as near as they could get to Azelot. Scurrying ground staff, who had witnessed the aftermath of some rough scraps, were appalled by the old men who sat drained of all but blood in the gashed cockpits. An experienced observer said it was the worst show he had been on.

The *Jastas'* final mad fling was reserved for 10 de Havillands from 99 Sqn after they had noted bursts on the workshops at Bühl. The adjacent village had been evacuated, which was as well because most bombs fell near cottages alongside the Bruderdorf-Saarbrücken road. Twenty interceptors climbed like lifts and another vicious battle ensued. A Nine spun off but recovered enough to be flown back carefully. Lieut A. T. Bowyer and wingmates saw the crash of 'his' Hun, Lieut Burrows destroyed a second, and the third poured smoke after bursts from Tremellen.

In France the 7th was dud; as was the 8th. But under England's bleak sky 15 flyers were chosen while fitters and riggers climbed long ladders and examined three Super Handleys . . .

Ten DH 9As were due for collection by 99 Sqn but it was still a test machine that Capt Sanders flew to shake up railways and motor transport beyond Château Salins the following morning. Major C. R. Cox, AFC, the latest CO, and Lieut L. B. Duggan piloted others, two 230-pounders and three 112-pounders dismaying the *Eisentruppen*. Cox, quickly establishing himself as one of the rare 'flying COs', understandably lost his way but carefully landed at Toul with his bombs intact.

Five out of six DH 4s circling Bensdorf station did likewise because the target was obscured; and three out of five from '104' also failed at Lorquin and Réchicourt, due to weather or recalcitrant Pumas.

In England 15 men were briefed, three Super Handleys petted and fed by fitters and armourers. A Rolls-Royce expert arrived and decreed that *all* the Eagle VIIIs on one machine must be changed. 'Stand Down' . . .

To the Deutz works at Cologne on the 10th went two flights of DH 4s, one machine straying from the formation so that 11 drove on over towns whose configuration grey cloud waves made unfamiliar. As they probed the brief open spaces for recognisable points they were jolted by a myriad of shells, and weave as he would the leader could not push through the fiery walls of successive boxes. Cologne was out of the question and Ehrang station took the bombs.

Fate was never more cruel to '55' than when a sliver of steel, despite the volume of *flak* the only palpable hit, impaled 23-year-old Capt 'Jock' Mackay. His DH 4 fell into a gentle glide, giving his observer, the irrepressible 2nd Lieut H. C. T. Gompertz—who, his Lewis drums expended, had once thrown a hammer at a Hun scout—the chance to slip in the emergency stick and with great nerve and judgment bring them in to a bouncy landing.

Eleven DH 9As from 110 Sqn and nine machines of '104' bombed Morhange airfield.

In England 15 men were briefed, three Super Handleys run up purposefully. The expert required all the engines on *another* machine to be removed. 'Stand Down' . . .

The evening gloom at Xaffévillers was brightened by a display of pyrotechnics on the horizon, an event that excited speculation about a Cease Fire. The celebrants were at 115's aerodrome where 2nd Lieut Cyril Box wrote in his diary: 'Surprised to see French troops, who had been passing up the road for days before, returning. Everybody wondered what was afoot . . . was the war over. There was a lot of premature excitement . . . Very lights were fired and there was great cheering but nobody had any accurate news.'

At Autigny Trenchard was no wiser. An Italian officer telephoned him to say the Armistice had been signed, but this he could not confirm.

In these circumstances the two duty crews from 100 Sqn were under peculiar stress when they took off for Lillingen and Frescaty aerodromes to deposit eight 112-pounders and 12 incendiary canisters. In similar case were two of 216 Sqn, one of whose bombs landed in the main street of Metz, killing five people and injuring seven. Single machines from 97, 115, and 215 bombed Morhange, where everyone must have been repenting his sins.

At about this hour the other '216' aeroplane was at Frescaty and voiding its squadron's last contribution to the war effort. Numbered 3127, it had the most remarkable record of any in the IF; for during a total of 400 operational hours its crews had earned two Distinguished Service Orders, two Distinguished Service Medals, a Distinguished Service Cross, a Distinguished Flying Medal, a *Medaille Militaire*, two *Croix de Guerre*, and a Belgian *Légion d'Honneur*.

Any of these raiders could have become a footnote in history, but by the RAF's 24-hour clock (introduced on October 28) the privilege of being the last to bomb German territory belonged to 100 Sqn—which had made the initial night raid for 41st Wing.

The finalists were Lieut Daryl E. White (pilot) of Seattle, 2nd Lieut P. Loftus of Newport (Co. Mayo), and 2nd Lieut A. E. Gwyther of Fleetwood; and Lieut G. Crocker (pilot) of Umberleigh, North Devon, 2nd Lieut W. H. Greaves of Essex, and 2nd Lieut W. K. Best of Wigan.

At Frescaty, to mark the retirement of the Independent Force, RAF, they left a blazing pyre.

* * *

In England on November 11, 15 men were briefed, the engines of three Super Handleys roared harmoniously, bombs were trundled out—1000 lb to a machine—for winching into the yawning maws. A signal arrived, this time from Lieut-Col Mulock. 'Armistice' . . .

* * *

No war ends tidily. A few sporadic outbursts of Verys, back-slaps, drinks all round, the wonderment of actually being able to marry the girl and find the village clock standing still at three; and the squadrons' routine, aimless now, was resumed.

At No. 115, which had finished operations with several pilots for every fit machine, Box was pleased that he could get flying practice, but—he was only 18—dismayed that he had not proved himself more over Hunland.

In the anteroom at '55' they talked of 'Jock' Mackay, expecting that his engine had conked, that he and Gompertz would soon walk in with armfuls of souvenirs. As they contemplated, Mackay died.

Recording Officers' files were being brought up to date, totals totted for forwarding 'through channels' so that Trenchard's staff could compile an account of his stewardship. It would be precise, informative, and—in Weir's word, 'educative'; an utterly official document of things attempted, things done. Except for the final sentences, whose untidy fervour carried the impression of Trenchard's personal pen...

'I would like to state here that the courage and determination shown by pilots and observers were magnificent. There were cases in which a squadron lost the greater part of its machines on a raid, but this in no wise damped the other squadron's [*sic*] keenness to avenge their comrades, and to attack the same target again and at once.

'It is to this trait in the character of the British pilots that I attribute their success with bombing Germany, as even when a squadron lost the greater part of its machines, the pilots, instead of taking it as a defeat for the Force, at once turned it into a victory by attacking the same targets again with the utmost determination.

'They were imbued with the feeling that whatever their casualties were if they could help to shorten the war by one day, and thus save many casualties to the Army on the ground, they were only doing their duty.

'I never saw, even when our casualties were heaviest, any wavering in their determination to get well into Germany.'

Now the Independent Force was not buoyant. In the forefront of all thoughts was the future, and to flyers unique in that they had laid the foundations of a discernible heaven in the midst of unimaginable hell, whose newly acquired skills had no ready outlet in the civilian's world, that looked bleak indeed. They had become vulnerable.

At least for four IF squadrons in the first frosty winter of peace there was a reprieve.

* * *

Speed was synonymous with postal delivery. From runner to steam packet mail organisations had striven to 'git thar fustest with the mostest'. A letter had been carried from Lyons to London by balloon in 1841 and 60 ascents with messages and packages made during the siege of Paris in 1870. Zeppelins undertook deliveries in 1909. English pioneer Claude Grahame-White flew aeroplane mail at Blackpool the following year; and in 1911 the Post Offices of Great Britain, the United States, India, South Africa, and France sponsored experimental air carriage.

Not until May 15, 1918, was the world's first official air mail service inaugurated, by the US War Department, over the 218 miles between New York and Washington. Europe's 'first' was established by French *Adjudant* Houssais, flying a twin-engined Letord bomber with patched bullet holes, who conveyed 50 letters and 10 lb of printed matter for American troops along the 230 miles from Paris to St Nazaire in three and a half hours.

Although termed 'regular' the services left much to be desired. They were flown by slow aircraft, at long intervals, and across country for the most part flat. They could not be regarded as either a true public service or as a sound financial proposition. Their continuance depended on pilots and machines and meteorologists who would beat every type of weather and navigational hazard.

The British looked to the one aviation body which, though not yet expert in sustained long-range, day-and-night, all-weather operations, was inured to their hardships.

The DH 4s, rear cockpits cleared for the canvas mail sacks, commenced the Occupation Mail runs on December 2, flying to Mons from St André-aux-Bois near Hesdin in northern France, a place familiar to 55 Sqn crews of Bloody April 1917 as Trenchard's old headquarters.

No. 99 also worked from St André and from Auxi-le-Château

and Aulnoye. From Maisoncelle went 110 Sqn, and from Marquise 216 Sqn.

The loads were 'official', up to 460 lb of troops' post and despatches per machine, and a principal route was to Cologne. The 9 Acks usually flew 229 miles in two and a quarter hours; and in fog 110's 'Tim' Armstrong, AFC—later a Senior Captain of British Overseas Airways Corporation—once hedge-and-house-hopped, rarely above 20 ft, for most of the journey. But come snow blizzards or pea-soupers all the pilots went.

By the following March they had completed 978 schedules, a record of 96 per cent success.

In the next six months the RAF mailmen made 1842 trips, accounting for 3000 hours' air time, 270 of them on a non-stop service from Folkestone (Hawkinge Aerodrome) to Cologne, a distance of 250 miles. Overall there was again a 4 per cent failure, due largely to faulty engines, although the new cross-Channel service completed 267 flights with 1 per cent failure.

Regularity was also good. Mails were delivered from Folkestone on 146 of the 182 days (80·2 per cent) and from Cologne on 139 days (76·4 per cent).

Here the IF's direct contribution to the air mail ended. But some pilots divined their destiny in aviation. They looked with speculative eyes on the RAF's passenger service from London to Paris and other Continental towns—934 people carried, three pilots and one passenger killed, at an average cost of 1s 0½d per mile. Once released from the Service they were willing recruits of monocled, swashbuckling, Sir Sefton Brancker, a former associate of Trenchard and the future Director of Civil Aviation. He had begun Aircraft Transport and Travel, a company which launched the world's first regular civil service, between London and Paris, on August 25.

Other companies, Handley Page Transport Ltd and S. Instone & Co Ltd, joined AT & T in the long-range stakes, all offering £400 a year plus 10s an hour flying pay to skilled bomber pilots. With these commercial venturers several IF veterans died—among them Bradley of the ice-clearing exploit on September 16, 1918, and his former Messmate, 'Froggy' Leroy. So, eventually, did the firms, bankrupted by public apathy and the crippling cost of the heavy-drinking wartime engines.

Immediately, then, those who managed to remain in the pruned Air Force fared better. In 216 Sqn they ran passengers and mail from Egypt to Palestine and Iraq, still on 0/400s; three years later inaugurating, with DH 10s and Vickers Vimys, the romantic Cairo–Baghdad Mail. No. 97, re-equipped with DH 10s in the summer of 1919, began Asia's first air mail between Bombay and Karachi.

Thus did the hawks turn into doves.

# PHASE IV

## *'What a Force it was!'*

# 10 *'For we are in danger to be called in question for this day's uproar . . .' (Acts 19:40)*

The port was circulating and they were reclining in the Savoy Hotel's wicker-backed chairs, the 'top table' in RAF blue tunics, and others in the civilian's new braid-edged evening dress. It was June 14, 1919, and though Prince Albert, an RAF officer well acquainted with Azelot, was the principal guest they had come to hear the well-remembered boom of a 46-year-old General with a racking migraine headache.

At last Trenchard rose to propose the toast of 'The Independent Force'—officially disbanded since the first weeks of the year.

They knew the figures by heart, would carry the human facts behind them through their lives, but just the same their former leader reminded them with some approximate totals[1]: More than 12,000 bombs dropped, representing 553 tons in 578 raids, and that not counting the work of the Force's forerunners. Decorations had been awarded to 151 flyers and ground staff, 74 officers and 77 other Ranks.

'What a Force it was!' he exclaimed. 'Absolutely unique in its character, and the only Force that has ever operated that was not Army or Navy but this new Air Force . . . Its spirit was to finish the war quickly and without any regard for your own safety.'

Disjointed phrases, confusing tense and number, littered with redundancies, as ever artlessly persuasive, exploded through the cigar haze:

'The one single purpose this Force had in view was that if you could help to win the war half a day earlier, even if you were all lost, your casualties were small compared with the overwhelming benefit of avoiding those enormous casualties to the Army fight-

1. See Appendix A.

ing on the ground,' he boomed in a sentence that was a triumph for his lung. 'And that is what we all felt—could we save and help the Army and our great infantry on the ground!'

Trenchard recalled his conviction that to bomb Germany would have been an expensive luxury until the Western Front squadrons were strong enough to contain the aviation opposing them and the soldiers. That ensured, it became a necessity. He also stressed the importance of round-the-clock operations.

'If night bombing only was done you lost half the effect of that night bombing and all the effect of day bombing on the morale of the nation we were hitting,' he continued. 'People were able to pursue ordinary avocations of the day; but if day bombers come people say "how disgraceful defences are, what funks the people are", and the result is they get more and more rattled.'

Everyone but the Press reporters, vainly trying to translate and yet preserve the flavour, loved it. Even as he spoke, however, the validity of his praise and assumptions were being examined by an Air Ministry Commission back from the rubble of factories, and transport and aerodromes.

Industrially, the inspection teams discovered a patchy picture of the Nancy group's activities. Blast furnaces, so easy to pick out, so difficult to hit in vital spots, were practically unscathed. At Burbach the cost of material repairs amounted to 488,000 Marks[1] (£24,800), at Dillingen £15,000, at Rombach £8500, and at Karlshutte £3300. Incalculable, but obviously more effective, was the constant stoppage due to *Flieger Alarms*, when furnaces cooled and produced flawed steel and less of it than was ordered.

Chemical plant, too, survived. The output of the Badische Anilin and Oppau works, for instance, did not diminish and any 'lost' time was quickly made up.

Munitions and heavy industries were in a sorrier state. Whole shops were found in ruins, buildings gutted; but these were merely the surface disturbances. A 20 lb Cooper, pitched awkwardly at a searchlight by an irritated rear gunner of a Handley Page, might crack a few hundred marksworth of machinery but the 'knock-on' effect of his bowling would disable an assembly line for days. Unexploded bombs further retarded production. Nor was an actual attack necessary.

Bous was bombed seven times during the entire war but it

1. Roughly equivalent to a shilling, the 1914 Mark's purchasing power was at least six times greater than it would be today.

had 293 alarms and output at the Mannesmann factory plummeted.

A typical balance sheet was that of the Röchling steel works of Völklingen, where there were 266 alarms. These caused an output deficiency of 20,031 tons, 4327 complete gun carriages, 1364 shells of 21 cm calibre, and 140 of 7·7 and 10 cm calibre. An assessment of total bomb damage reached £5890, but when able to check their calculations the surveyors invariably found that everywhere they had underestimated.

The Röchling repair bill in October 1917, for example, they put at £2900 when it was actually £3600 and that of the following February at £8 4s instead of £53.

In August there was no raid, but 50 alarms caused a deficit of 2881 tons, the loss of 780 gun carriages, and 229 shells. The interesting aspect of these figures is that they were double those for March 1917. Then there were three raids and six false alerts attributable to 3 (RNAS) Wing and French partners who inflicted far worse material damage on the plant.

The moral effect of the IF must have been considerable for at that factory there were plentiful raw materials and no labour shortage.

Doubtless the workers were in poor fettle. Through the summer of 1918 the period of probable night attacks extended from 8.30 pm to 4.30 am—a wider time range than was generally open to the London-raiding *Luftwaffe* of World War II—and the management was forced to pay danger money which fluctuated with the number of alarms and the pay-roll.

The tally for 1917 was October (17 alarms) £1300, December (4) £90; 1918, January (11) £520, February (11) £490, March (8) £240, April (1) nil, May (13) £770, June (33) £1050, July (47) £1050, August (50) £1500, September (44) £1820, October (23) £800, and November (4) £190—a total of some £9800 which produced nothing but short tempers.

Money was also cascading in workers' compensation, chiefly for nervous ailments. Doctors noted that a few minor bomb casualties brought an influx of 'exhaustion' cases and malingerers. Under pressure from *bürgermeisters* and company directors the Government finally decreed that claims for compensation of less than £755 were to be paid immediately. Where this was not obeyed with alacrity executives, especially at Saarbrücken and Ludwigshaven, had to cope with protest meetings. The Board of the Ludwigshaven Badische works said the financial loss amounted to £205,000, £78,000 being paid to legitimate casualties and dependants, 23 workpeople being killed and 62 injured including five permanently crippled.

Bombs and *flak* splinters accounted for £100,000. Interruption of trade, production loss, and 'sheltering the homeless', however, was placed at the unexpectedly low sum of £25,000.

The manager of a Lorraine metallurgical centre said raid-induced strikes caused an average monthly loss in output of 10 per cent; and in Luxembourg German iron foundries had been reduced to between a half and two-thirds of their 1913 quota. Shortage of coke and transport was the main reason. Much of that the IF had waylaid in transit. But the Air Ministry Commission also learned that whenever a factory hand was killed his workmates refused to finish their shift—'so the loss of output is as great as when important material damage is done'.

Protection of a positive kind had not been easy for plant employees to find. Many shaped molten metal, and carried out maintenance under suspended chassis, boilers, and gun barrels, and filled shells in rooms which were barely splinter-proof.

At Bous a dummy works, erected 100 metres to the north-east of the Mannesmann complex and equipped with lights, may once have deceived the Independent Force. Two bombs fell on it, but just as possibly they were badly aimed at the real factory. Another dummy at Frankenthal, 100 metres long and 200 broad, had a glass, illuminated, roof and was meant to decoy raiders from the Badische works. It failed.

Although Boards complained when the Government did not protect their shareholders' investments they were not anxious to contribute to the upkeep of balloon barrages near the works. With some justification they believed them ineffective and, anyway, had no desire for a balloon collapsing and its steel cable smashing chimneys or tearing off roofs.

Ostrich-like mayors, too, resented the siting of AA guns near industrial premises, convinced that they brought harm to the town.

Landau was not bombed until May 1918. Light *flak* batteries moved in, and the town was visited twice. After the June 30 attack the *bürgermeister* declared:

'My own observations have led me to believe that the attack was not originally intended against Landau. Before any bombs were dropped I distinctly and repeatedly heard machine gun fire. It may therefore be assumed that the enemy airmen were driven off their real objective and pursued, whereupon, they got rid of their bombs in their hasty retreat.'

When confronted by such timidity—Wiesbaden was not alone —the workers naturally preferred to stay at home. Assuredly they did not want to be in the vicinity of railways.

Locomotives and repair shop had taken such a mauling that in the latter months every seriously damaged engine was either 'reduced to produce' or abandoned. Several locos bombed in the autumn of 1917 were unrepaired two springs later. Mangled rolling stock, which had been a favourite IF target because of Germany's limited amount, lay strewn alongside mile upon mile of track.

At Metz trucks had been broken up to serve as roofs and anti-blast walls for dugouts. Stores of repair equipment had become ashes and in any case there was no labour to spare.

Railway stations were only moderately damaged, apparently having been patched up expeditiously because no experts were needed; but also to disguise from the public the situation in the outside 'yards'. The permanent way, although perpetually twisted and dislodged, had been quickly replaced so that traffic flow was not seriously affected from that cause.

More frequently transport dislocation stemmed from the *Flieger Alarms* which held up completely sound trains. Saarbrücken officials said the slightest alarm stopped traffic for two hours.

Militarily, the side-effects of Trenchard's campaign were plain for any soldier to grasp, be he the front line private trembling as he awaited his overdue relief, the machine gun officer ordering 'bursts of two' to conserve what little ammunition remained, or the Staff colonel denied reserves posted to protect the 'civvies'. By 1918 maybe half the German fighting army was in the top medical categories. In the summer Haig's Armies captured many who had been rejected as unfit even for light duties two years before. The old men and boys of the *Landwehr* were useful for hunting shot-down crew, but of necessity the *Eisentruppen* had to be formed from thoroughly tough fellows drawn from active service units. *Flak* and *scheinwerfer* specialists could be ill-spared, but nevertheless their Western Front ranks were thinned.

Within a month of the IF getting into action crews of 386 heavy AA guns, 153 searchlights, and 62 machine guns were attempting to guard the Moselle Valley, Saar Valley, Palatinate, and the zones of Kreusnach-Mainz, Cologne-Bonn-Coblenz, and Frankfurt, with 40 men to a heavy piece.

Comparable figures for autumn are not extant, but the vast transfer of arms to Home Defence can be gleaned from a resumé of protection afforded individual areas:

| | *guns* | *searchlights* | *m/guns* |
|---|---|---|---|
| Essen (not raided) | 80 | 74 | — |
| Cologne | 126 | 66 | 26 |
| Frankfurt | 77 | 16 | 6 |
| Diedenhofen (Thionville) | 121 | 103 | 52 |
| Saarbrücken | 81 | 63 | 36 |
| Mannheim | 84 | 38 | 32 |
| Freiburg | 99 | 34 | 10 |
| Stuttgart | 74 | 41 | 16 |
| Munich (not raided) | 42 | — | 4 |
| | 784 | 435 | 182 |

Two hundred aeroplanes and aviators, reckoned by Trenchard's Staff, was a conservative estimate of the number held back from tactical work. It would include the 10 *Kests* and perhaps four reconnaissance and bomber squadrons. In fact by September several *Jastas* were also involved, and experienced pilots at advanced flying schools were being retained either to stiffen the aerodrome Defence Flights or as *Kest* replacements.

Thousands of pioneers were continually engaged on repairing airfields, building new ones, and in levelling areas for emergency or 'relay' strips.

Shelters, too, took weeks to construct. At Boulay they were of concrete, seven feet high and with walls 18 inches thick. Bühl had a similar arrangement. Morhange fared less well, comfort seeming to take precedence over security. Here the dugouts were 200 ft by 20 ft, divided into cosy rooms, but with earth-packed roofs propped on wooden struts. One was pierced easily by a bomb.

Sometimes the toiling builders grew tired, or rebellious, and they sank other Morhange dugouts so far and sited the drainage pipes so carelessly that the shelters were immediately flooded and stayed that way.

The most intriguing riddle for the Commission, however, was the moral imprint of the Independent Force. The German Government obliged only with bald facts, the key one being the summation of ascertainable loss from aeroplane raids, French and British, on German soil throughout the war—23,500,000 Marksworth (£1,175,000) of material damage, 720 killed and 1754 injured. Gothas and Giants had killed 8136, injured 1972, and inflicted £1,418,272 worth of damage in Britain.

But at the outset of their enquiries, made among ordinary folk as well as officials over the whole IF 'front', the investigators established that any resemblance between the British and German raids was superficial.

In the first place the Fatherland was running down. It had shared the blood baths of the Somme and Third Ypres with the British, its peasant allies were thinking too much about their poor harvests, and the mounting intervention was a topic for conversation around any board table or cold hearth. There was, too, a subversive undercurrent of native-born Communism, swelling imperceptibly to break the feudal dam as its tributaries had in Russia.

These oppressive matters impinged on the ordinary German, but the Royal Navy's denial of his food and heat was a daily worry. The country cousin with his eggs and wood chips was the prosperous one; and even he could be brought low by the Flanders Fever.

The figures of the *bürgermeister*, lager-paunched, top-hatted, Kaiser-moustached, and voluble, loomed large over the ruins, whether they amounted to acres of blasted factory or a hole in the wall of a cottage on the outskirts of his domain. He was the personification of such independence from the military regime as the townsman might enjoy. In the street he stepped aside for a German officer to pass without inconvenience, but in the town hall his voice rose in fustian protest and, amplified by its many fellows throughout the State, echoed to Berlin.

As a people's spokesman he accepted with reasonable grace temporary defeats, stalemates, and the 'unfair' naval blockade, offset as they were by the tangible victories and the bombing of Allied capitals—which he understood to suffer severely. But for the IF breaking up his doorstep no *bürgermeister* would have credited that German supremacy could be a myth. Once shown that there was no stopping the bombers he questioned other doctrines and finally doubted the wisdom of the sacrifice.

He also noted the rapid exodus of the industrial emperors who were sowing and harvesting the battlefields, and that reports of London raids had ceased; and he heard the unquenched rumours of an American bombardment programme.

Then it was that he reverted to being a Bavarian, a Saxon, a Westphalian, an Alsatian, a man of his State, and invariably one with a grudge against the more militaristic Prussians and their overbearing *Junkers*. His anger destroyed the other German myth, that of a united Fatherland which was the basic reason for the Kaiser's existence.

In the military block of the capital's Wilhelmstrasse the Army had always spared some contemptuous thought for the *bürgermeister*, a petty official useful for a patriotic speech. But, pricked by the Reichstag to whom they felt the vacillating Wilhelm II paid too much heed, they had to divert a disproportionate quantity of their energies, men, and arms to beating off flies. The fact that their own States were under fire was of no moment. Why should civilians not share the soldiers' danger?

When the Air Ministry men discussed morale in the target towns three months had gone by since a bomb hit Germany. The French had demanded swingeing reparations, handfuls of marks were needed to buy milk or an egg, and though embittered ex-officers execrated everyone but the Army from any *bierkeller* or street corner platform, the Germans realised that unless a miracle occurred their future was mortgaged to the Allies. They were in their 'umble mood. Yes, they agreed, the bombing had been frightful but . . . that's war, *nicht wahr*?

Wrote the Commission: '. . . The average German probably believes, as he was always instructed to believe during the war, that this method of warfare was adopted in self-defence . . . Very few cases of bitter feeling with regard to air raids were observed.

'The question "who did it first?" is probably more frequently discussed than the problem of moral justification. The German mind can easily improvise some plausible justification for an undertaking which is crowned by success.

'Seeing, however, that the supreme justification is here lacking in his own case, the tendency is to deny it to himself and his adversary alike and to seek to let the matter drop as quickly as possible.'

Undoubtedly the IF had greatly diminished the civilians' spirit as Haig, Salmond, and Jellicoe had broken the resistance of the soldiers, airmen, and sailors.

In his memoirs General von Ludendorff, German Army Chief of Staff, relates the Supreme Command's gloom in September when it 'would not permit the employment of a specially effective incendiary bomb' (the two-pound magnesium Elektron which ignited on contact, could not be extinguished by water, and was designed to start another Great Fire of London) 'because of the reprisals which were to be expected against our own cities'.

Whether the Force's moral over material effect was as Trenchard expressed it, '. . . in a proportion of 20 to one', was not then a paramount issue. Years later it would be.

Indisputable was the unstinted courage and enterprise of its flying men, the unflagging loyalty and dexterity, both mental and physical, of the ground crews. Had they been unwilling to maintain their exertions they would have wasted the strategical concept as well as the tactical practices.

The weather was unkind enough to them, bringing about the complete abortion of 13 raids, the partial failure of 72. The misbegotten Puma and legitimately strained engines caused the early return of outward-bound aeroplanes on 346 occasions. After unlucky pilots had experienced three or four of these mishaps in a month they could not blow and hold up a column of mercury in a U-tube, the Stress Test originated by Martin Flack, physiologist of the RAF Medical Research Department.

Afforded such determination Newall and Trenchard might have achieved more obvious results. But their ration of machines was meagre even when not unduly defective. By November 11, 41st Wing had 59 machines on charge, 83rd Wing 49, and 88th Wing 32 (including 45 Sqn's Camels and lately received Snipes).

Newall began with 46 (10 night), progressed to 64 (28 night). That was also the quota of the IF until August 9 when it became 84 (30 night, 100 Sqn converting to the Handley Page Battle Order of two five-machine Flights). On August 19 the number was 94 (40 night), and at the month's end 122 (50 night). At no time was every machine available and during five periods an entire day squadron, with an official strength of 18 aircraft, was out of action.

Spread over winter, spring, summer, autumn, and winter again there has never been a more awesome test-to-destruction of an

RAF group, and this when it was the sole representative of a unique, untried, and, in some spheres, unwanted organisation.

The accomplishments were substantial and, allowing for the putrid weather inevitably ahead, these foundations would have been decked impressively. Leaving aside the 'shuttle service' the Handley Pages would have been fitted with two Jenkins belly lights, angled so their beams converged on the ground at the moment for release of the bombs. This device—next used, so far as is known, by Avro Lancasters on the Möhne Dam raid of May 1943—permitted low and consequently accurate drops. Additionally it provided a safety factor over undulating terrain. Ordinary bombing would be effected by the new Course-Setting Bomb Sights with inbuilt compasses.

In Lieut-Col Landon's Wing there was a tentative scheme for landing saboteurs to set fires on German aerodromes. One o/400 had been fitted with fuselage ladders to facilitate their exit and December 10, under the next bright moon, had been fixed for the first attempt.

Logically evolved, that type of warfare would have meant the IF supplying weapons to Lorraine and Luxembourg where, once encouraged, agents could speedily have formed Resistance 'cells' and supplemented the bombers' industrial destruction. Billy Mitchell's airborne infantry need not have been far behind.

By the spring Snipes and Martinsyde Buzzards would have been escorting day bombers such as the fast DH 10. Wireless telephony between cockpits and formations was ready, as were Morse telegraphy receivers through which late weather news could be passed from Base.

There was no likelihood of parachutes being issued—'unsafe and likely to undermine a proper offensive attitude' was the official reason, to which Trenchard mistakenly subscribed—but self-sealing tanks were in prospect.

All these moves the IF could have initiated alone. Its impact as the IAIAF spearhead would have been irresistible. HP, Vickers Vimy, and Caproni casualties from the enemy's two-seater night fighters would not have been light, but means of detection and control were too primitive for any meaningful victory in the Battle of Germany. The Siemens Schuckerts and Fokker D8 monoplanes would gradually have displaced the Albatros and Pfalz during daylight. These, however, could be of small avail against the locust swarms the New World factories would ensure.

Nor might the Germans, unlike the 16th-century English facing the Spanish Armada, pray to God he would blow with his winds and scatter them. By their nature air armadas could be rebuilt. By the law of averages they would find more fine days than foul.

Everything was ready. But the *coup de grâce*, in the light of history much needed, was no longer wanted.

# II *'How shall we escape, if we neglect so great salvation . . .' (Heb. 2:3)*

The Independent Force had lost a few battles but had won a campaign. Was it then possible for strategic bombers to win a war? That was the question which was to tease politico-military pundits until the atomic rocket made their discussion as pointless as whether enough fire-ships could have driven an 18-century maritime nation to capitulate.

All the answers lay in the Force's record and in the words of their commander. Some were in fact extracted and employed to further momentary designs and desires of individuals. Others were adopted long-term without translation to period.

But during the vital inter-war years their overall pattern was lost in a welter of Service squabbles and irrational political directives.

Despite Jutland, the Great War had left the Royal Navy unable to contemplate any conflict in which it was not the dominant element. To make quite sure, it demanded the return of its air arm. The Army, ruefully accepting that it needed the co-operation of airmen rather than horses, had an able rearguard fighter in Colonel Repington—'No evidence has been given that the Independent Air Force shortened the war by an hour . . . It is a heresy for Sir Hugh Trenchard to suggest that the air force can be a substitute for part of our garrison overseas . . .'

The Royal Air Force, its squadrons shrunk from 96 to 23 (and only 10 of those serviceable) in the post-Armistice retrenchment, with the 1920 Air Estimate the equivalent of a fortnight's expenditure in 1918, was again a Cinderella and one whose virtue her old sisters took every chance to doubt. Trenchard, back as Chief of Air Staff for 10 years, outfought the Repingtons, soothed the Treasury by his thrift, and designed the Service in his image.

He overhauled the training of permanent officers, instituted short-term commissions, established the Halton School for engineering apprentices—personally securing the entry of its most valuable graduate, jet-engine pioneer and Air Commodore Sir Frank Whittle—and created a civilian reserve in the Auxiliary Air Force.

With successful punitive actions in the Middle East and India he demonstrated how aircraft could preserve the lives of British soldiers and their foes alike while saving the taxpayers' money. Pre-radar he developed scientific 'early warning' systems, and the Larynx guided missile with a range of 200 miles—whose progress ended abruptly with the Government's refusal of £1,000,000 for further experiments.

Regrettably, almost fatally, he had no opportunity before his retirement to activate a strategic bomber organisation. Some observers have construed this omission as proof that Trenchard had little belief, always supposing he had ever had any, in industrial attacks. But in what became known as his Last Will and Testament, a summary of faith for Cabinet guidance, the IF's role was to him the decisive element in 'The Future Employment of Air Power in Imperial Defence'. His first task, accomplished, had been to save the RAF as an entity. Minute budgets, internecine strife, political havering, and now age had prevented completion of the mission.

The doctrine he bequeathed was that unlike the army the Air Force did not have to defeat the opposition in the field. The entire wealth of the foe 'from boots to battleships' was the bomber's legitimate prey, and 90 per cent was made or stored in cities.

Rather than take an entrenched machine gun at the cost of a platoon he would smash it in its box hundreds of miles from the men it was built to maim. A proportion of bombs would stray and kill civilians who had subsidised the machine gun. In strictly military terms that would be wasted, but wherever an enemy house collapsed there, too, morale would be harmed, time and money and manpower spent in clearing the debris.

That was the way to avoid another Somme, another Passchendaele.

With the departure of this unique man—soon to revolutionise London's police—the RAF again became a plaything of peace-pledging politicians. Wilfully blind when not moral cowards, these soothesayers held back development of the aircraft industry by economic strictures and the propaganda associated with eight years of futile Disarmament talks. By sticking to the 1924 'Ten Year Rule', which assumed that in that period no major war would be possible, they deferred provision of even 52 squadrons from 1928 to 1936. Surely it was a feeble Air Council which allowed them to ignore the passage of the years.

Ostensibly the planners were firmly behind the theory of Counter Offensive; but their record from 1929 to 1935 reveals that they took few practical measures to implement it. Stanley Baldwin, Lord President of the Council, told the House of Commons in July 1934 that the defences of England were on the Rhine; but the two bomber squadrons supplied for every fighter squadron were mostly 'mediums' and useless for a strategic role. They were housed in Hampshire, Wiltshire, Berkshire, and Oxfordshire, on the assumption that France would be the next enemy. Somehow Bircham Newton had escaped the Treasury axe and a couple were put there.

Had the Air Marshals vehemently adhered to the precepts of the IF, absorbed the analyses of its deployment, and applied its tactics intelligently to the requirements of their time the Air Council of the early thirties might well have prevailed.

The feeling that, except when strategic bombers were called in question as an integral part of the Royal Air Force, they did not protest the validity of counter-offensive with solid conviction is inescapable. In the whole period after Trenchard's departure Sir Cyril Newall, formerly of 41st Wing, was the only man in high office to have practical knowledge of the IF. Until his term as Chief of Air Staff, from September 1937, the majority of senior officers, with the 'regular' Air Force in 1918, had inevitably acquired a tepid attitude to squadrons divorced from the tangible needs of the armies. Others were ex-Navy and under the mental burden of ties made in formative years.

Counter-offensive was a convenient emotional tag to justify the RAF's existence as a separate service; but professionally it was the least appealing of all the air roles to career officers inured to a 'support' function.

Thus in the thirties Britain probably failed to halve the duration of the war and indeed almost lost it. It was Newall who threw out the schemes for seeking a precarious parity with the Luftwaffe's supposed strength. He demanded numbers based on a calculation of the RAF's minimum strategic necessity. This included 1442 first-line bombers to be completed by the summer of '41. Part of this commitment would be four-engined machines, which had twice the range and 10 times the bomb load of the twin-engined so-called 'heavies' then coming into service.

Even then the Government refused to alter the pace of peacetime industry and rejected the plan, although, in emasculated form, it remained on the books until Hitler annexed Austria. It was then replaced by a Striking Force complement of 1352 aeroplanes by March 1940. The Munich Crisis decreed another alteration, to 1360, but with the depressingly far-off completion date of March 1942.

Subjected to the stop-go treatment the RAF none the less did manage to revive the IF, under the title of Bomber Command. Created on July 14, 1936, this force, whose instructions also encompassed tactical functions, had 33 operational squadrons by World War II. Nos. 99, 110, 115, and 215 were there. Nos. 55 and 216 were in Middle East Command, '97' and '104' had become aircrew 'pools' and '100' were flying torpedo bombers. When things became rougher they were recalled to the fold.

It was the youthful ingenuity and integrity of men like Newall, Charles 'Peter' Portal, Edgar Ludlow-Hewitt, and Wilfrid Freeman that gave their country its eventual strategic capability in suitable bombers, air and ground crews of impeccable standard, and a remarkably mature headquarters structure.

They were not ready at the deadline; but then they did not control the factories. Nor was the RAF's own account debit-free. Some errors might be of an ancillary nature but between September 1939 and 1943 they postponed Bomber Command's strategic fulfilment.

* * *

In the autumn of 1918 the heaviest bomb in regular use weighed 1660 lb; the heaviest available, 3300 lb. Twenty years later the heaviest in service was 500 lb, bomb bays customarily held 50, 100, and 250-pounders and the explosive power had increased little.

The Course-Setting Bomb Sight, essentially that of 1918, was still standard. Apart from parachutes, sanctioned officially in 1927, and the recent replacement of Lewis guns by the Vickers

K gas-operated type or the Browning belt-fed ·303, offensively the long-distance men were no better equipped than their fathers had been.

Near Heligoland on December 18, 1939, the fate of 10 burnt offerings out of 24 Vickers Wellingtons brought home this deplorable fact to the Air Staff. Air Vice-Marshal John Baldwin, then Air Officer Commanding 3 Group, commented on the disaster: 'Many of our aircraft were observed during and after combat to have petrol pouring out of their tanks . . . The vital necessity of fitting self-sealing tanks to all bombers cannot be overemphasised.'

His other conclusion, derived from his experience with VIII Brigade, was less tenable. The Wellington leader had set too hot a pace, causing two of his flights to straggle. Therefore Baldwin urged that the closest formation consistent with safety be kept. But his Wellingtons' maximum speed of 235 mph against the Messerschmitt Bf 109E's 355 mph compared unfavourably with the DH 9's 85 mph against an Albatros D 5's 117 or even a Fokker D 7's 130.

The attackers, *Jadgeschwader* I (Richthofen's Own), reported that bunching helped them because they could fly rings round the mass, picking their firing angles at will, and avoiding the devastating four-gun tail turret—with which the Air Marshals had believed bomber formations could fight their way through.

Evidently the first of the IF's lessons, *day bombers need fighter protection*, had been ill-digested. Nothing could be done at that late hour, no long-range escorts had been envisaged; and an appalled Command had to eschew the critical pattern of Trenchard's 1918 operation—*night bombing must be complemented by day bombing*.

After the retreat from Dunkirk, Churchill, echoing Trenchard but equally adhering to his own 1917 definition of strategic bombing, voiced the task before Bomber Command:

'The Navy can lose us the war but only the Air Force can win it . . . Fighters are our salvation but the bombers alone provide the means of victory. We must therefore develop the power to carry an ever-increasing volume of explosives to Germany so as to pulverise the entire industry and scientific structure on which the war effort and economic life of the enemy depend . . . In no other way at present visible can we hope to overcome the military power of Germany . . .'

Its dependence on nice navigation and pinpoint bombing invalidated that policy, for not even by 1942 had the scientists perfected press-button methods of pathfinding.

When the War Cabinet recommended the use of parachute mines, World War II's first obviously indiscriminate weapon, a professionally outraged Air Council insisted that it concentrate on 'precision' targets. But its faith was simple indeed. Only the Americans possessed a precision sight for daylight work as only US day squadrons could now ensure Allied *regular, sustained, attacks round the clock,* which the IF had essayed and periodically achieved on its own.

Optimistic crew reports, a method of damage assessment which Trenchard rarely accepted without visual aid, had deluded Air Intelligence for months. Over a year 49 per cent of bombs in south-west Germany, the IF's happy hunting ground, had fallen on open spaces. In June and July 1941 only one in 10 aircraft bombed within five miles of any Ruhr target.

Once it was acknowledged, internally, that nothing the size of a factory could be hit with certainty at night Bomber Command was handed over to Air Chief Marshal (later Marshal of the RAF) Sir Arthur T. Harris who, quite incidentally, in the twenties had introduced the prone posture for aimers and cut down his squadron's 'bombing error' from 200 to 20 yards. He also accepted a fresh policy, six months' concentration on 'the morale of industrial workers in west and north-west Germany'.

Officially that was not yet area bombing, but, as never before, there was some substance in the Germans' use of the term *terror flieger*. The IF had, of course, cracked German morale in places and, what was more significant, upset the people's *conduct*. But that had been achieved against a Fatherland weary and ill-nourished, not one fed by half of Europe, maintained by slave labour, and chained to the Gestapo dogs of a homicidal psychotic. Besides, not until the following year could the loosely escorted Americans penetrate Germany.

Consequently the Allies' Casablanca Conference of 1943 yielded another directive for Harris and USAF General Ira C. Eaker:

'Your primary object will be the progressive destruction and dislocation of the German military, industrial, and economic system, and the undermining of the German people to a point where their capacity for armed resistance is fatally weakened.'

Inspired by Portal that was practically a repetition of the strategic part of Foch's plan for the Inter-Allied Independent Air Force.

There was one politically motivated clause—'Berlin . . . should be attacked when conditions are suitable for attainment of specially valuable results, unfavourable to the morale of the enemy and favourable to that of Russia.'

The last five words set a precedent for the controversial 1945 order to bomb refugee-choked Dresden in the path of the Russian tanks. That apart the clock had at last been turned back to the autumn of 1918.

From July 24/25 the Command and the 8th Air Force began four round-the-clock raids on tinder-dry Hamburg, culminating on the 27/28th in a fire-storm, in which air heated to 1000 degrees Centigrade created typhoon-like suction that uprooted trees and razed small buildings. Damage was 75 per cent non-industrial, but 25 per cent of the work force was off the pay-rolls. By the bestial mathematics of war that put area bombing well into the black.

But again an IF maxim was ignored: *Stoke the fires periodically and systemically.* Hamburg was left relatively undisturbed for a year and quickly restored its capacity.

Night intercepters did not engage Trenchard's men and, seeing that Halberstadts did attack 0/400s in the north of France, there is reason to suppose that the IF's anti-aerodrome ploy had rendered them incapable. Earlier in World War II Fighter Command had some successes when on 'Rhubarbs', their name for strafes, they shot up Occupied airfields. Their brief, however, did not correspond with the IF's interpretation of *keeping the Hun's head down.*

By mid-'43 550 night intercepters were in full cry above the Reich; but *Luftwaffe* units, also neglecting the IF axioms, did not intrude in substantial numbers on British bases, although in the March 1945 death-throes a party cornered returning bombers over England and shot down 19 of them with ease.

Had that sort of enterprise been encouraged Harris's loss rate —averaging 4·2 per cent by moonlight in 1942 and later rising on some missions to 6 per cent—would have become untenable. Thanks to Trenchard's defensive-offensive the *Luftstreitkräfte* had been kept too busy to strafe his fields with precision or consistency, and from June 5 to November 11, 1918, no IF machine was destroyed on the ground by enemy action and very few, and those by day, when flying on our side of the Lines.

With the advent of the Halifaxes and Lancasters capable of hauling bomb loads up to 22,000 lb the doom of Germany's chief cities was only a matter of successive blows. Many industries were dispersed, but these were isolated by the cutting of their lifelines.

Previously 'Bomber' Harris had considered accurate bombing of railways and yards to be beyond his Command—this despite the shape and strength of 'shops' and tracks having changed fractionally since the IF had disrupted Metz and Thionville with tiny explosives.

In the last quarter of 1944 a greater weight of bombs fell on Germany than throughout the previous year. General bombing, precision as well as area, in the final phase illustrated Trenchard's contention that given sufficient means and skill air power could bring an industrial nation to its knees.

The valour of Bomber Command crews needs no poet; neither does the endurance of their operational commanders, who bore the mental torture of sending thousands of men into the breach several times a week for years on end—a responsibility to which leaders of no other arm were exposed.

But to blossom from the seeds Trenchard had planted two decades before, the Command of 1939 needed fertilisers; at least 500 four-engined bombers . . . heavy bombs . . . sights suitable for high-flying machines . . . night navigation aids for fast ones . . . long-range escorts for daytime . . . even enough oxygen points to prevent crews collapsing. These tools would not have prevented Germany sweeping the BEF from France or forcing the RAF to win the Battle of Britain and hive off bombers for the Battle of the Atlantic. But early in 1941 Bomber Command would have been established as the principal offensive arm and recognised as industry's 'No. 1 priority'.

In so far as it affected Britain at this juncture Germany's might stemmed chiefly from her predatory U-boats, and these were vulnerable—as soon they would not be in specially constructed concrete pens.

Germany itself was comparatively ill-defended, Goering having assured a people already flying victory flags that no enemy bomber could cross the Reich; and a tattoo of savage day-and-night attacks conceivably could have started a landslide. But there were no heavyweights and an attempted KO would have snapped the RAF's stringy right arm.

'As the enemy conquered Poland and France by their tank blitz so we can smash the German machine by the bomber blitz,' Trenchard declared in 1940. He saw no impediment to the War Cabinet using 'the great alternative' to the sacrifice of millions on a conventional war dominated by soldiers.

Long away from the right Corridors he could not know with what sadness his disciples were compelled to deny him.

## TOUCH DOWN

Late on May 30, 1942, a four-engined Short Stirling of 218 Sqn, one among 1046 aircraft, set off from Marham in East Anglia on a 300-mile trip to Cologne. The captain was a South African, Wing Commander Paul Holder, and in the second pilot's seat was a former Wing Commander.

Before they reached the city they saw a bomber explode like a flare. As they toggled from 16,000 ft a Hun fighter came in from starboard, but turned on to another bomber in the stream.

Dodging the *flak* from 500 guns and the beams of 130 searchlights the Stirling made for home. Ninety miles from the target it completed a slow circuit so that all the crew could contemplate the pulsing globule of fire that denoted the RAF's first 'thousand bomber raid'.

At 3.30 am the wheels kissed the runway. Stripped of flying kit the second pilot joined the rest at briefing, and everyone marvelled at the braid on his tunic sleeves.

Twenty-four years to the month after his beloved '55', Air Vice-Marshal 'Jack' Baldwin had been to see for himself.

## APPENDIX A

# The Score

The squadrons, as the RFC/RNAS 41st Wing, RFC/RAF VIII Brigade, or RAF Independent Force, were on operations for 396 days.

They undertook: 650 MISSIONS, including 172 attacks on the German homeland. Of these 508 were bomb raids—51, individual efforts—and 142 photo-reconnaissances.

Pre-IF there were 55 day and 87 night raids, all the day and 54 night attacks being on industrial objectives. Different targets amounted to 156.

According to a statistically suspect statement made by Trenchard in 1919 these involved one 'raid' (perhaps 'aeroplane flight' was meant) of 50 miles, 51 of 100 miles, 101 of 150 miles, and 151 of 200 miles. By the same reckoning the IF—which made 205 day and 373 night raids—flew 325 'raids' of 50 miles, 142 of 100 miles, 70 of 150 miles, and nine of 200 miles. Whatever the basis for the list it indicated the extent to which semi-tactical co-operation with the Armies interrupted the IF's strategic work.

In the IF period flying HOURS—practice, air test, and operational—were apportioned as follows:

| | DAY | NIGHT |
|---|---|---|
| June 6–30 | 1515 | 399 |
| July | 1768 | 767 |
| August | 2019 | 846 |
| September | 1605 | 761 |
| October | 1828 | 629 |
| November 1–11 | 661 | 109 |
| | 9395 | 3511 |

Examples of record round-trip DISTANCES are:

| | DAY | NIGHT |
|---|---|---|
| June | 272 | 240 |
| July | 272 | 300 |
| August | 330 | 342 |
| September | 320 | 272 |

BOMBS dropped throughout the 13 months came to 1,491,588 lb (665 tons, 17 cwts, 3 qtrs), pre-IF machines delivering 2370 bombs weighing approximately 107 tons in total, the IF contributing 12,514—390 tons at night. Aerodrome strafes absorbed 220¼ tons.

The loads were made up of:

| *Number* | *Type* |
|---|---|
| 11 | 1600/1650 lb |
| 54 | 550 lb |
| 837 | 230 lb |
| 9902 | 112 lb |
| 21 | 50 lb |
| 266 | 40 lb |
| 3820 | 25 lb (Coopers varied, between 20 lb and 25 lb, as did weights in the SN range) |

In addition 816,019 baby incendiaries were used.

To the nearest ton the monthly weight dropped by the IF was: June, 57; July, 88; August, 101; September, 179; October, 98; November, 20.

A number of 'missing' aircraft toggled before being brought down but the weight they carried was not added in by RAF book-keepers.

IF PHOTOGRAPHIC crews exposed 3914 plates, only one machine being destroyed by enemy action while so employed. Plate expenditure by months was: June, 748; July, 845; August, 704; September, 946; October, 584; November, 87.

CASUALTIES in all flying operations amounted to 419:

| | | | |
|---|---|---|---|
| *killed* | pilots | 15 | 50 |
| | observer/gunners | 35 | |
| *missing* | pilots | 138 | 298 |
| | observer/gunners | 160 | |

| | | | |
|---|---|---|---|
| *wounded* | pilots | 29 | 63 |
| | observer/gunners | 34 | |
| *injured* | pilots | 11 | 28 |
| | observer/gunners | 17 | |

These figures were compiled from Wing records in December 1918. Dealing only with the IF the Official History gives 'personnel casualties' as 29 killed, 235 missing, and 64 wounded. That reckoning cannot have been easy, because RAF Routine Orders of June 27, 1918, changed the nature, and validity, of Returns: 'In future strictly flying accidents resulting in death will be reported as death in action. Injury resulting from accidents will be reported as "sick".'

By this means the inexperience of pilots and the unreliability of aeroplanes was disguised.

Neither accounting takes cognisance of aviators and ground crew strafed by Hun raiders or blown-up in bomb mishaps. But the butcher's bill is appalling enough.

Assuming that the IF's final nine bomber squadrons had each had an operational 'day' establishment of 36 aircrew all would have suffered more than 100 per cent casualties. Actually, the Handley Page units had fewer men, most did not appear before the final quarter, and the German defences were less effective at night. Which is why we find 104 Sqn, for instance, having to close-down three times, and sustaining losses amounting to at least 250 per cent.

The all-important factors in survival prospects, training and battle experience, are illustrated by the veteran 55 Sqn, which lost 18 machines in 49 industrial raids, and the fledgling 110 Sqn, which was virtually shattered in five.

The mental anguish endured without respite by COs during the long daylight hours of summer can be gauged from two 'readiness states' of 99 Sqn. Available for the Sqn's first 'show' on May 20 were:

| | *pilots* | *observers* |
|---|---|---|
| 'A' Flight | W. D. Thom (ldr) | L. G. Claye |
| | E. L. Doidge | W. B. Walker |
| | N. S. Harper | D. G. Benson |
| | C. S. Johnson | T. K. Ludgate |
| | O. Jones | E. Beale |
| | K. D. Marshall | O. Bell |
| (spare) | W. G. Stevenson | T. W. Wiggins |

| | | |
|---|---|---|
| 'B' Flight | P. C. Purser (ldr) | R. F. Connell |
| | H. Sanders | W. W. A. Jenkin |
| | E. A. Chapin | B. S. W. Taylor |
| | V. Beecroft | N. T. Melville |
| | W. J. Garrity | M. A. Skinner |
| | S. M. Black | E. Singleton |
| (spare) | J. W. Richards | E. J. Munson |
| 'C' Flight | A. D. Taylor (ldr) | H. S. Notley |
| | D. A. MacDonald | F. H. Blaxhill |
| | C. C. Conover | ? |
| | M. T. S. Papenfus | A. L. Benjamin |
| | R. F. Freeland | R. E. Sothcott |
| | H. D. West | J. Levy |
| (spare) | F. G. Thompson | S. C. Thornley |

By July 25 the line-up (asterisks denoting 'originals') was:

| | *pilots* | *observers* |
|---|---|---|
| 'A' Flight | *Thom (ldr) | *Melville |
| | *Doidge | *Walker |
| | *Stevenson | J. K. Speed |
| | *Marshall | *Bell |
| | G. Broadbent | J. Jones |
| | *West | M. A. Dunn |
| (spare) | C. D. Clark | A. T. Bowyer |
| 'B' Flight | *Beecroft (ldr) | *B. S. W. Taylor |
| | *Garrity | *Beale |
| | Wilson | F. L. Lee |
| | C. W. Hewson | H. E. Alsford |
| | *Black | *Singleton |
| | L. V. Dennis | F. W. Woolley |
| (spare) | T. M. Ritchie | L. W. G. Stagg |
| 'C' Flight | *A. D. Taylor (ldr) | *Notley |
| | *Papenfus | *Benjamin |
| | *Richards | *Munson |
| | G. Martin | S. G. Burton |
| | F. Smith | K. H. Ashton |
| | P. Dietz | H. W. Batty |
| | (no spare available) | |

Officers had been switched around the Flights to become leaders and deputies or to uphold the practice of 'experienced pilot, new observer' and vice-versa. But a week later Doidge, Walker, Melville, Burton, Dietz, Batty, Dennis, and Woolley were dead; Ritchie, Stagg, Black, Singleton, Papenfus, Benjamin, Garrity, G. E. Stephenson prisoners; and Martin wounded.

Such was the state of pilotage, engines, and aerodromes that more than twice as many AEROPLANES were crashed as were destroyed by EA or *flak* or by technical failures over enemy ground. Altogether the squadrons 'wrote off' 458, types and quantities being:

| | *missing* | *wrecked* |
|---|---|---|
| HP 0/100 & 0/400 | 23 | 58 |
| FE 2b | 11 | 49 |
| FE 2c | — | 7 |
| DH 4 | 33 | 70 |
| DH 9 | 52 | 102 |
| DH 9A | 18 | 29 |
| Sopwith Camel | 1 | 3 |
| Sopwith Snipe (7F 1a?) | — | 1 |
| BE 2c (GHQ Communications) | — | 1 |
| | 138 | 320 |

On the other side of the ledger were 64 EA destroyed—which meant they had to be 'broken up in air, on fire in air, seen to dive steeply and *reach* ground in this manner, or to have pilot fall out'. Victories less certain were those claimed over 93 'driven down out of control'.

APPENDIX B

# The Squadrons

DAY

55 Formed at Castle Bromwich, Warwickshire, April 27, 1916. Equipped as bomber unit at Lilbourne, Northants, January 1917. Two months later started active service at Fienvillers.

Under Newall and Trenchard made 130 bombing raids and dropped 97 tons. Claimed 15 EA destroyed, 32 out of control, 21 'driven down'. Lost 24 aircraft; had 13 aircrew killed, 36 missing, 14 wounded. COs: J. E. A. Baldwin, 11.10.17; A. Gray, 7.1.18; B. J. Silly, 20.9.18.

99 Yatesbury, Wiltshire, August 15, 1917. Mobilised as bomber unit at Ford Farm, near Salisbury, a fortnight later. Arrived St Omer, April 1918. Made 76 raids, dropped 61 tons. Seventy-nine per cent of its aircraft bombed allotted targets. Claimed 12 EA destroyed and seven out of control. Lost 21 machines in action. Six aircrew killed, 42 missing, 16 wounded. Nineteen crew were 'posted' permanently for various forms of unfitness. COs: L. A. Pattinson, 3.5.18; P. E. Welchman, 23.9.18; W. D. Thom, 29.8.18; C. R. Cox, 5.11.18.

104 Wyton, Huntingdonshire, September 4, 1917. Mobilised at Andover, Hants, late September 1917. Reached St Omer May 1918. Made 31 raids on industrial objectives, dropped over 41 tons. Destroyed 30 EA, shot down 27 out of control. Re-formed three times because of casualties —5 killed, 66 missing, 24 wounded. Lost 33 machines. CO: J. C. Quinnell, 20.5.18.

110 Rendcombe, Gloucestershire, November 1, 1917. Mobilised at Kenley, Surrey, in June 1918. Made five industrial raids, dropped 10½ tons (33 × 130 lb and 145 × 112 lb). Claimed one EA destroyed, 10 out of control, and five 'driven down'. Seventeen aircraft missing, 28 wrecked. One killed, 34 missing, four wounded. CO: H. R. Nicholl.

NIGHT

97 Waddington, Lincolnshire, December 1, 1917. Moved to Stonehenge in January and to Netheravon, Wiltshire, July 1918. Arrived France the following month. Flew 91 bomb raids, dropped 64 tons (including three 1650-pounders). Fired 20,680 rounds at ground targets. Had six killed, nine missing, and one wounded. CO: V. A. Albrecht.

100 Hingham, Norfolk, February 1917, with Home Defence Wing crews. Arrived Izel-le-Hameau, April 1917. With 41st Wing and IF made 91 industrial raids and at one period operated on 13 nights consecutively. Dropped 213,219 lb—including two 1600-pounders. Destroyed three EA. Five killed, 17 missing, three wounded. COs: M. G. Christie, 11.10.17; W. J. Tempest, 11.12.17; C. G. Burge, 16.6.18.

115 Catterick, Yorkshire, December 1, 1917. Mobilised at Castle Bromwich near Birmingham, July 1918. Reached France in August. Made 15 raids and dropped 26 tons. Best mission was against Morhange when five HPs, making two trips apiece, released 6½ tons. First raid, 16/17 September, when four tons were dropped on Metz, was described by Trenchard as 'the finest piece of work which has ever been done by a new squadron'. Casualties—1 wounded; 3 missing (these being on an HP forced down by AA fire in Luxembourg). CO: W. E. Gardner.

215 Coudequerke, near Dunkirk, on March 10, 1918, as 5 Sqn, RNAS. Re-formed at Netheravon in April it was mobilised at Andover, Hampshire, in July and joined the IF on August 19. Made 16 industrial raids and dropped about 3500 bombs. Lost 30 aircrew and had two wounded. CO: J. F. Jones.

216 Originally an anti-submarine unit with Flight strength, operating from Redcar, Yorkshire, it was re-formed as 'A' Sqn, RNAS, at Manston, Kent, on October 5, 1917. Reached France five days later. Made 162 raids on 66 nights and dropped 176½ tons—including four 1650-pounders. Eighteen crew were lost in industrial attacks, two others wounded, and at least 12 aircraft destroyed. COs: K. S. Savory, 17.10.17; H. A. Buss, 28.1.18; W. R. Read, 1.9.18.

APPENDIX C

# The Tools

BOMBS

*20/25 lb Cooper Mk I.* Amatol filled, one detonator. Basically a heavy-steel cased fragmentation bomb for use against transport, aerodromes, and personnel. Four fitted to each underwing rack and dropped in 2, 3, 4, 1 order by Bowden cable release. They were held in tumbling triggers, these in turn being held by locking studs. Nose and tail supports stopped bomb from rocking and projections either end prevented the fusing vane from rotating during flight.

*40 lb Incendiary.* Bulbous, with tail fuse and trigger tied to rack by string. Phosphorus mixture loaded through hole in nose, then sealed in by wooden plug. 'Set' on a timing ring to explode 700 ft above target. *Baby Incendiaries* were also released from canisters or thrown from cockpits.

*112 lb RL Mk I.* TNT or amatol, with fulminate of mercury detonator and tetryl exploder. Cast steel casing, four wind vanes. Cartridge in tail fuse could delay action after impact from ¼ to 15 seconds.

*230 lb RFC Mk III.* Light case, producing craters. Nose armoured for maximum penetration. Filling was 40/60 amatol, delay up to 15 seconds. The *550 lb RL* was similar, with four detonators and two exploders.

HOLT FLARE

Comprised four sticks of 'rocket compound' attached to a Japanese parachute. It was placed in the Electric Launching Tube, inclined 20 degrees under fuselage, and set off by spring contacts near the muzzle. The flare was supposed to fall 10 ft before igniting and drifting downwind.

### HIGH ALTITUDE DRIFT SIGHT MK I A

Instructions for use:

(1) Set sights level.
(2) Set height on arc scale, which automatically sets movable foresight.
(3) Find airspeed from pitot (ASI) reading.
(4) Fly at right angles or left angles to wind according to height and pick up fixed object on ground. Turn out drift bar until object is parallel to it. This automatically sets ground speed and up-and-down wind sight.
(5) Turn at right angles to wind and see that horizontal and vertical bars are in correct position.

### WILLIAMSON L CAMERA

Semi-automatic, its exposure mechanism being driven by wind. Housed in bay aft of observer and cradled vertically in a sponge rubber frame to absorb vibration. Lens cones of from 4 in. to 20 in. focus on $5 \times 3\frac{7}{8}$ in. plates, the largest cone projecting beneath the machine and wired to prevent the slipstream shifting it. Crews often disconnected the wind vane, which iced-up easily, and worked the 'L' by hand, the pilot sighting and triggering, the observer loading plates. In a later version, the 'LB', lugs guided the plates—which fell by gravity alone—and prevented jams.

### COMPASS COURSES

As set for 115 Sqn, Roville.

| *Target* | *Distance* (*mls.*) | *Bearing* (*true*) |
|---|---|---|
| Hagenau | 73 | 13 degrees |
| Karlsruhe | 109 | 174 |
| Mannheim | 117 | 59 |
| Metz | 30 | 357 |
| Saarbrücken | 52 | 43 |
| Saarburg | 40 | 84 |
| Speyer | 112 | 64 |
| Thionville | 45 | 357 |
| Trier | 76 | 13 |

## APPENDIX D

# The Opponents

| *Type* | *Engine* | *Speed (max.) mph* | *Climb (loaded) mins.* | *Ceiling (service) feet* | *Arms* | *Bomb Load pounds* | *Duration hours* | *Remarks* |
|---|---|---|---|---|---|---|---|---|
| ***British*** | | | | | | | | |
| DH 4 | RR Eagle III | 119 | 36·40/15,000 ft | 16,000 | 1 V* 1/2 L | 4 x 112 2 x 230 | 3½ | Extra tanks and reduced bomb load put up endurance to 5½ hours. |
| | RR Eagle VIII | 143 | 16·30/15,000 | 22,000 | ” | ” | 3¾ | |
| DH 9 | Siddeley Puma | 111·5 | 45/15,000 | 15,500 | 1 V 1/2 L | 3 x 112 2 x 230 or equiv. | 4½ | Run to unstick, 112 yards. Landing run (engine off), 160 yds. |
| DH 9A | Liberty 12 | 123 | 33/15,000 | 18,000 | 1 V 1/2 L | 2 x 230 3 x 112 | 5¼ | Up to 660 lb bomb load possible. |
| DH 10 Mk III 'Amiens' | 2 High Compression (405 hp) Libertys | 124 | 34·20/15,000 | 16,500 | 4 L | Up to 900 lb | 5¾ | 1½ lb pom-pom fitted as experiment in nose. Dual control rear cockpit. |
| FE 2B | 160 Beardmore | 80·5 | 16·38/6000 | 11,000 | 1 L | Mixed, up to 350 lb | 3 | FE 2c, little used, had observer in rear but a similar performance. |

| *Type* | *Engine* | *Speed (max.) mph* | *Climb (loaded) mins.* | *Ceiling (service) feet* | *Arms* | *Bomb Load pounds* | *Duration hours* | *Remarks* |
|---|---|---|---|---|---|---|---|---|
| HP 1/100 | 2 Eagle II | 86·5 | 30·30/6500 | 7000 | up to 6 L | 16 x 112 | 8 | 4/6 Coopers for throwing by rear gunner. 2 x 112 could be carried under fuselage. |
| 0/400 | 2 Eagle VIII | 97·5 | 27·10/6500 | 8500 | | 16 x 112<br>3 x 550<br>1 x 1650 | 8 | |
| HP V/1500 | 4 Eagle VIII (in tandem) | 97 | 18·30/6500 | 10,000 | 4/6 L | Up to 30 x 250 | 6 min.<br>14 max. | Designed to carry one 3300 lb bomb. Berlin raid max. 1000 lb. Six delivered by Dec 31, 1918. |
| Vickers FB 27 'Vimy' Mk IV | 2 Eagle VIII | 103 | 33/6500 | 7000 | 2/3 L | 2 x 230 plus 18 x 112 | 11 | One made first non-stop W–E Atlantic crossing, 1919. |
| Sopwith F1 Camel | 130 Clerget | 113·5 | 15·50/15,000 | 24,000 | 2 V | (for strafes) 4 x 25 | 2½ | Top-scoring scout of war. Once carried 1 x 112 lb bomb. |
| Sopwith 7F1 Snipe | 150 Bentley II | 121 | 18·50/15,000 | 19,500 | 2 V | (for strafes) 4 x 25 | 3 | Official title for production a/c, Snipe Mark I. |
| Tarrant Tabor Triplane | 6 x 450 Napier Lion (4 in tandem) | 110 | 33·30/10,000 | 13,000 | ?8 L | 40 x 112 or equiv. | 8 min.<br>12 max.<br>(at 91 mph average) | Intended for IAIAF in 1919. One built; crashed on test May 26, 1919. Power-assisted controls. Performance figures are engineers' estimates. |

| | | | | | | | | |
|---|---|---|---|---|---|---|---|---|
| *American* | | | | | | | | |
| Liberty Plane (DeH 4) | Liberty 12 | 124 | 14/10,000 | 15,800 | 2 Ma 2 L (or 2 B) | 12 bombs (up to 322 lb) | $2\frac{1}{2}$–3 | Wireless, camera, Holt flares for night photography. |
| *French* | | | | | | | | |
| Breguet 14B2 | 300 Renault 12Fcx | 110 approx | 47/16,500 | 19,000 | 1 V 2 L | 32 x 115 mm ($17\frac{1}{2}$ lb) or equiv. | $2\frac{3}{4}$ | Bombs in Michelin wing racks dropped by observer. Dual control, armoured seats. |
| Spad XIII | 220 Hispano-Suiza 8BA | 128 approx | 18·30/16,405 | 22,300 | 2 V | — | 2 | Range 200 to 250 miles. |
| *Italian* | | | | | | | | |
| Caproni Ca. 3 | 3 x 150 Isotta-Fraschini | 85 | 60/9800 | 10,000 | 4 R | Up to 3000 lb | ?4 | Day bomber intended for night work with IAIAF. |
| *German* | | | | | | | | |
| Gotha G.IV | 2 x 260 Mercedes D IVa | 87·5 | 28/9840 | 14,500 | 2/3 P | 660 lb (England: usually 6 x 50 kg) | $3\frac{3}{4}$ min. 6 max. | G-V, found around Nancy, had slightly better speed, slower climb. |
| Hannover CL IIIa | 180 Argus As III | 103·12 | 5·3/3280 | 24,600 | 1 M 1 P | Grenades | 3 | Wireless, camera. |
| Rumpler C VII 'Rubilt' | 240 Maybach Mb IV | 109 | 50/22,960 | 23,900 | 1 P | — | $3\frac{1}{2}$ | 100 mph at 20,000 ft. |
| Albatros D V | 160 Mercedes D III | 103 | 35/16,500 | 20,000 | 2 M | — | 2 | |

| *Type* | *Engine* | *Speed (max.) mph* | *Climb (loaded) mins.* | *Ceiling (service) feet* | *Arms* | *Bomb Load pounds* | *Duration hours* | *Remarks* |
|---|---|---|---|---|---|---|---|---|
| Fokker DR 1 Triplane | 110 Oberursal UR II | ?115 | 15·30/16,400 | 20,000 | 2 M | — | 1½ | |
| Fokker D VII | 160 Mercedes D III | 114 | 38·5/16,400 | 19,600 | 2 M | — | 1¾ | |
| | 185 BMW | 125 | 16/16,400 | 22,900 | | | | |
| Pfalz D III | 160 Mercedes D III | 102·4 | 41·20/15,000 | 17,000 approx | 2 M | — | 2–2½ | Built by three Everbusch brothers at Speyer, near Mannheim. |
| Siemens Schuckert SS D III | 160 Siemens Halske Sh III | 112·5 | 13/16,500<br>20/19,680 | 26,000 approx | 2 M | — | 2 | |

* Arms: B—Browning; L—Lewis; M—Maxim; Ma—Marlin; P—Parabellum; R—Revelli; V—Vickers.

# Selected Bibliography

## Chronicles


*War in the Air* (vol 6) H. A. JONES OUP 1937

*Per Ardua* H. ST. G. SAUNDERS OUP 1944

*Civil Defence* (History of the Second World War) T. H. O'BRIEN HMSO & Longmans, Green & Co 1955

*The War Illustrated* (8 vols) Amalgamated Press 1914–18

*History of the Great War* Waverley Book Co Ltd 1914–19

*1918: The Last Act* BARRIE PITT Cassell & Co Ltd 1962

*The Great War* Amalgamated Press Ltd 1914–18

*The Doughboys* LAURENCE STALLINGS Harper & Row Inc 1963

*Royal Air Force 1939–45* (3 vols) DENIS RICHARDS AND H. ST. G. SAUNDERS HMSO 1953–55

*Flying Corps Headquarters 1914–18* MAURICE BARING William Heinemann 1920

*The Central Blue* SIR JOHN SLESSOR Cassell & Co 1956

*The Third Service* SIR PHILIP JOUBERT Thames & Hudson 1955

*War Memoirs of Lloyd George* Odhams Press 1938

*Aerial Wonders of Our Time* Amalgamated Press n.d.

*Air Bombardment* SIR ROBERT SAUNDBY Chatto & Windus 1961

*Bomber Squadrons of the RAF and Their Aircraft* PHILIP MOYES Macdonald 1964

*Bombers* C. G. GREY Faber & Faber 1942

*The First Battle of Britain* RAYMOND H. FREDETTE Cassell & Co 1966

*Raiders Approach* SQN LDR H. T. SUTTON Gale & Polden Ltd 1956

*The Thousand Plan* RALPH BARKER Chatto & Windus Ltd 1956

*Bomber Offensive* SIR ARTHUR HARRIS Collins 1947

*The Forgotten Ones* SIR PHILIP JOUBERT Hutchinson 1961

*Into the Blue* NORMAN MACMILLAN Duckworth 1929

*The Military Intellectuals in Britain* R. HIGHAM University Press, New Jersey 1966

*The Franco-Prussian War* MICHAEL HOWARD Collins 1960

## Biographical

*Trenchard, Man of Vision* ANDREW BOYLE Collins 1962

*Heavenly Adventurer* BASIL COLLIER Secker & Warburg 1959

*To Know the Sky* PRUDENCE HILL William Kimber 1962

*The Mad Major* CHRISTOPHER DRAPER Air Review Ltd 1962

*General Billy Mitchell, Champion of Air Defense* ROGER BURLINGAME McGraw-Hill Book Co 1952

*Pioneer Pilot* WILLIAM ARMSTRONG Blandford Press 1952

## Technical

*The Shape of the Aeroplane* JAMES HAY STEVENS Hutchinson 1953

*Airplane Photography* HERBERT E. IVES J. P. Lippincott Coy 1920

*Practical Flying* MAJOR W. J. MCMILLAN Temple Press Ltd 1918

*History of Air Navigation* ARTHUR J. HUGHES G. Allen & Unwin 1946

*Aircraft of 1914–18* Harleyford Press Ltd 1954

*Reconnaissance & Bomber Aircraft of the 1914–18 War* Harleyford Press Ltd 1960

*British Aeroplanes 1914–18* J. M. BRUCE Putnam 1957

*German Aircraft of the First World War* PETER GRAY AND OWEN THETFORD Putnam 1962

*Encyclopaedia of Aviation* SQN LDR C. G. BURGE Sir Isaac Pitman 1935

## Records

*Entwicklung und Einsatz der Deutsches Flakwaffe und der Luftschutzes im Weltkriege* Ernst Siegfried Mittler, Berlin 1938

*Abschiesse Fiendlicher Flugzeuge und Ballone im 1917–18* Official German log

*The Annals of 100 Squadron* C. GORDON BURGE Herbert Reiach Ltd 1919

*History of 99 Squadron, 1917–18* L. A. PATTINSON W. Hepper & Son Ltd 1920

*The Chronicles of 55 Squadron, RFC & RAF* 'LM' (L. MILLER) Unwin 1919

*Bomber Command* Air Ministry & Ministry of Information 1941

*Report of Air Ministry Commission Into Results of Air Raids on Germany* 1919

## Periodicals

*Aeronautics* (July–Dec 1919), *Aeroplane* (1917–18), *Flight* (1917–18), *Popular Flying* (1932–38), *Flying* (1938–39), *Air Stories* (1938), *Cross & Cockade* (Journal of World War I Aero Historians), *Air Pictorial, Flying Review International*. (*Aircraft*) *Profiles* 5, 9, 25, 26, 31, 43, 50, 55, 62, 86, 97, 121, 157 (Profile Publications Ltd)

## Newspapers

*Daily Express, Daily Mail, Daily Sketch, Daily Telegraph, The Times; Sunday Pictorial, Sunday Telegraph.* Various German newspapers, generally mentioned in text. Also personal records 1938–67.

# Index

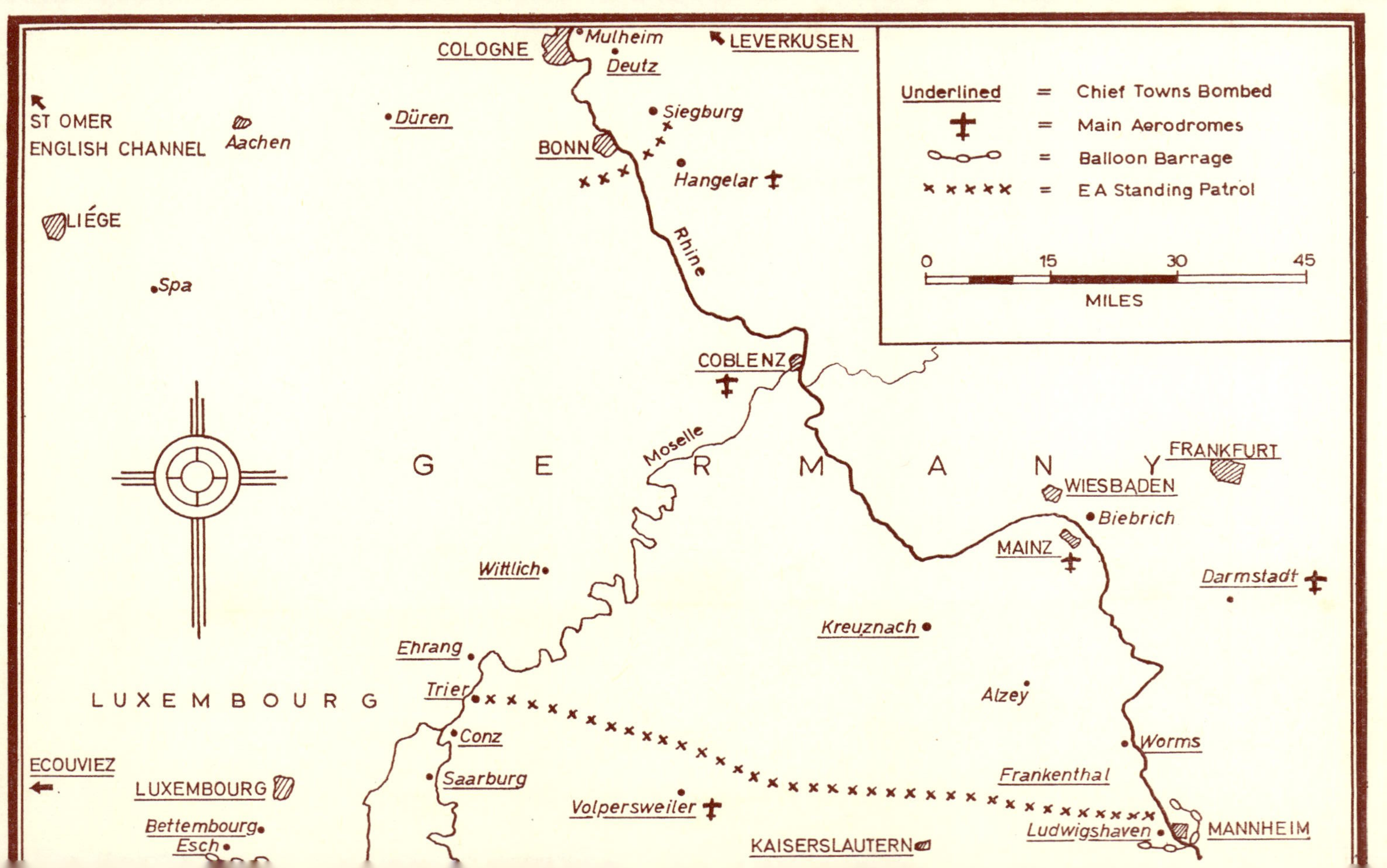

COLOGNE
Mulheim
Deutz
LEVERKUSEN
ST OMER
ENGLISH CHANNEL
Aachen
Düren
Siegburg
BONN
Hangelar
LIÉGE
Spa
Rhine
COBLENZ
Moselle
G E R M A N Y
FRANKFURT
WIESBADEN
Biebrich
MAINZ
Darmstadt
Wittlich
Kreuznach
Ehrang
Trier
Alzey
LUXEMBOURG
Conz
Worms
ECOUVIEZ
Saarburg
Frankenthal
LUXEMBOURG
Volpersweiler
Ludwigshaven
MANNHEIM
Bettembourg
Esch
KAISERSLAUTERN
Underlined = Chief Towns Bombed
= Main Aerodromes
= Balloon Barrage
××××× = E A Standing Patrol
0 15 30 45
MILES